Brian Lancaster is Senior Lecturer in Psychology at Liverpool John Moores University, where his research encompasses both brain science and the psychology of religion. His work on religion has focused on Judaism and he has lectured extensively on Jewish themes, both in the UK and Israel. He is the author of *Mind, Brain and Human Potential*, for which he was awarded the 1992 book prize in Science/Psychology by the Scientific and Medical Network.

The *Elements Of* is a series designed to present high quality introductions to a broad range of essential subjects.

The books are commissioned specifically from experts in their fields. They provide readable and often unique views of the various topics covered, and are therefore of interest both to those who have some knowledge of the subject, as well as those who are approaching it for the first time.

Many of these concise yet comprehensive books have practical suggestions and exercises which allow personal experience as well as theoretical understanding, and offer a valuable source of information on many important themes.

In the same series

THE ELEMENTS OF
JUDAISM

Brian Lancaster

ELEMENT
Shaftesbury, Dorset ● Rockport, Massachusetts
Brisbane, Queensland

© Brian Lancaster 1993

First published in Great Britain in 1993 by
Element Books Limited
Shaftesbury, Dorset SP7 8BP

Published in the USA in 1993 by
Element Books, Inc.
42 Broadway, Rockport MA 01966

Published in Australia in 1993 by
Element Books Limited for
Jacaranda Wiley Limited
33 Park Road, Milton, Brisbane 4064

Reprinted 1995

Cover design by Max Fairbrother
Typeset by The Electronic Book Factory Ltd, Fife, Scotland
Printed and bound in Great Britain by
Biddles Limited, Guildford & King's Lynn

British Library Cataloguing in Publication
Data available

Library of Congress Cataloging in Publication
Data available

ISBN 1–85230–402–2

CONTENTS

For my parents, Pearl and Gay, on their 50th
and my daughters, Kalela and Esther

An element of continuity in Israel

INTRODUCTION: THE MEANING OF SACRED HISTORY

The history of Judaism is at one and the same time the history of a religion and of a people. It is indeed a long and fascinating history. This book, however, is not primarily about history. I have chosen to try to convey something of the sense of Judaism as a living religion; to explore the spiritual insights which Judaism holds for the contemporary seeker. It is certainly true that Judaism has been forged through the crucible of history and that it is impossible to understand fully the religion divorced from its historical context; indeed, Judaism fundamentally believes that God has manifested Himself through history and that its own spiritual core derives from the historical encounter between the Jewish people and God. There are, however, two crucially different approaches to history. One is the literal, or academic, approach; the other seeks the sacred in history. 'Literal history' is thus to be distinguished from 'sacred history'. The literal history of Judaism and the Jewish people is not the primary subject of this book. Unless, however, one is infused with a sense of the validity of sacred history, one will be unable to enter into the profound vision of Judaism. The strong tendency for the modern mind to dismiss sacred history as at best having only a kind of poetic validity is, in fact, the major block to an understanding of the real place of religion in today's world.

Judaism unfolds at the intersection between the two forms of history. As a culture it binds a people in the dimension of literal history. As a religion it binds them into the altogether other dimension of sacred history. Such is the covenantal relationship to the divine which lies at the heart of Jewish consciousness.

Sacred history empowers the individual. It enables the individual to forge a living relationship with the events chronicled, since those events are not literally past. Time for sacred history is not the everyday passing time of literal history, but that mysterious dimension of time which is eternally present. In the same way that many fail to see the truth of sacred history, so do many fail to witness this other dimension of time. To reject the eternal present is, however, to close prematurely our account with reality. Whilst literal history may satisfy the rational mind, there are deeper dimensions to the psyche for which sacred history can provide an equally satisfying picture of the way things really are.

The Hebrew Bible is Judaism's source of sacred history. The Torah – the five books of Moses – comprises the essence of that sacred history. As one forges one's relationship with the Torah, so the true meaning of sacred history unfolds. For Judaism, there is much more to Torah than stories and laws alone. It does not merely relate a saga which is spiced with the spiritual basis of Jewish identity. Torah is the mystical source of all spiritual nourishment. The study of its words becomes to sacred reality what scientific analysis is to literal reality – it is a method for exploring the laws and intricate features of that reality.

Judaism does not ignore the rational mind. Far from it. Its tradition strongly emphasizes the fullest use of logic in the explication of the words of Torah, particularly concerning the various laws and their applications in the world. But the sense of sacred history is superordinate. The rational mind is, as it were, harnessed in the service of sacred history.

Many of the ideas explored in this book are illustrated

from the great post-biblical works of Judaism, its Talmud and works of Midrash. These mark the transition of Judaism into the form in which it is known today. The huge sweep of biblical history culminated in the Temple-based religion in Jerusalem. The rabbis whose views are chronicled in the Talmud and Midrashim were able to project Judaism forward into its post-Temple phase which has lasted now for almost two thousand years. The traditions of elucidating both the meaning of the Hebrew Bible and the details involved in fulfilling the laws of the Torah have continued throughout this period. Whilst there have been other major developments, for example in philosophy and mysticism, the basic orientation of Judaism hardly changed since talmudic times until Reform movements became established in the nineteenth century. Modern Orthodox Judaism continues to uphold the rabbinic orientation and rejects the break from tradition represented by Reform. It seeks to project the rabbinic orientation forwards into the foreseeable future.

Central to the sacred history of Judaism is the notion of exile. The theme of being 'strangers in a strange land' and of being ruthlessly persecuted has been repeated over the ages. What may be seen to literal history as a sad example of the callousness of humanity, becomes in sacred history a picture of the mission of Judaism in the world. It is significant that the Jews have been seen by many as the conscience of the world. Judaism bears a message which strongly extols ethical values. The key formative influence on Judaism was itself connected with the value of freedom – the release of a whole nation from bondage in Egypt. Judaism bears witness that no-one should be forcibly enslaved to another.

The heart of Judaism's message is the concept of monotheism. The notion that the universe is ruled by an ultimate, all-powerful Being has become familiar. But the message of monotheism also has a deep psychological meaning which many fail to appreciate. The mind comprises disparate elements, many of which are – in modern terms – unconscious. The thrust of monotheism is to bring unification, and therefore order, to these diverse elements. Indeed, Judaism's mystical teachings convey details of many meditative techniques directed specifically towards such unification. These may take the form of attempting to unify God's name, for example. Whilst the focus of such techniques is necessarily cosmic in scale, their role in promoting inner integration lends them a potent relevance to issues explored in contemporary psychology.

It is in this context that the importance of the prohibition against idolatory – a third pillar of Judaism's core teaching – should be understood. Again, many perceive only the outer skin of this teaching. Fundamentally, 'bowing down' to some tangible entity means granting power to something which is not infinite. Endemic to human psychology is the tendency to project power outwards onto figures who thereby become mythic in status. This may involve a real person (Hitler, for example) or an object or statue. Monotheism, coupled with the prohibition against idolatory, is a guard against this dangerous human tendency. Ideally (and, of course, human frailty means that the ideal is not always achieved), no identifiable image is granted powers beyond those which it realistically bears. In psychological terms, if an image becomes inordinately powerful through projection, it will act as a block to any higher psychological integration. Judaism strives to avoid the glorification of any image. Its ideal is that the individual's inner, psycho-spiritual world should mirror the external world itself, in which order is maintained by a higher, transcendent and infinite presence. Such an ideal does not come about simply by articulating some kind of creed. The path is one of active participation, involving not only belief but also intense practice. Most people classed as 'religious' adhere to the outward dimension of a religion only. My comments here concern more especially the inward, and the esoteric, dimensions.

Judaism conveys an outlook which is consonant with a vision firmly fixed in contemporary knowledge. My comments above have touched on modern psychology, and Jewish teachings can also be shown to be relevant to issues in modern physics and ecology, for example. My final chapter will return (partially) to literal history in order to examine these claims. But the relevance of Judaism to the challenges of our day may be seriously examined only through a deep consideration of its teachings. Judaism does not wear its insights on its sleeve. Moreover, for various cultural reasons, many features of its outlook are considerably misunderstood. In particular, many people see Judaism through glasses which have been tinted by Christianity and the western enlightenment. It is largely in an attempt to challenge these misunderstandings that I have written this book.

I cannot claim that a definitive account of Judaism is contained in these pages. Inevitably, in a work such as this there is a degree of selectivity, and my own biases must shine through the selections I have made. My major claim is to have attempted to enter into the wisdom of Judaism to such a level as to be able to convey its relevance to those who may be searching for spiritual meaning in an age of transition. To anyone who senses something of that wisdom, it will hardly need emphasizing that I have barely scratched the surface. There is always more to learn . . . .

I have included a glossary which explains all Hebrew terms used in the text. An appendix discusses the Hebrew alphabet and the Name of God. It also includes a table of the Hebrew alphabet. In a few places in the text reference is made to the significance of Hebrew letters. Indeed, many insights within Jewish thought are difficult to convey without referring to the original Hebrew. Readers lacking knowledge of Hebrew will, I trust, find the appendix adequate for this purpose.

Finally, I should like to acknowledge the part played by all those who have guided me in my own study and practice of Judaism. In particular, thanks are due to Rabbi Baruch Horovitz of Jerusalem and David Shaw of Liverpool for making helpful comments on an early draft of this work. I should stress that responsibility for all views expressed (and any errors) in this work rests with myself. A chance encounter in the Athens Synagogue resulted in some help with illustrations, for which I am grateful. I wish also to thank my wife, Irene, whose grasp of the issues I have tried to express has enabled her to make an invaluable contribution.

1 · An Outline of Jewish Belief and Practice

Shimon the Righteous ... taught: On three things does the world stand – on Torah, on divine service, and on acts of kindness [charity].[1]

What is distinctive about Judaism? All religions are concerned with our relation to the transcendent in one form or another, and Judaism is no exception. For Judaism, though, it is not faith or contemplation that cements the relationship, but *action*. Moreover, as the words of Shimon the Righteous – a sage from around 200 BCE – make clear, it is not merely the human soul that is the object of our religious actions, but the world itself. A pillar of Jewish belief is that humanity is partner to God in maintaining the world, not simply in today's fashionable sense of ecological responsibility, but in the more mystical sense which views 'religious' action as affecting a hidden realm from which the world draws its very being.

Shimon the Righteous' words capture the central features of Jewish belief and practice, and therefore appropriately introduce this first chapter. In subsequent chapters, the deeper character of Judaism will be explored through examining the principles on which these beliefs and practices are based. But here, I present a basic outline which will serve as a general and straightforward introduction to the question of Judaism's distinctiveness.

Study and Action

Shimon the Righteous has no need to describe the nature of God. Jewish belief about God (see below) is implicit in the practice of Judaism. Study and action define the path that leads to God. One knows God not primarily through philosophical or mystical speculation but through the study of His word – the Torah (Pentateuch), through prayer, and through the refinement of character that comes with giving charity, or, more generally, performance of deeds which promote harmony. The centrality of study to Judaism is truly a distinctive feature amongst world religions. In Chapter 2 we will examine in some detail Judaism's understanding of the Torah and the imperative to study its contents. In brief, study of the Torah is viewed as the means *par excellence* for reaching towards knowledge of God and His ways. It cannot be directly equated with the general view of study as being the intellectual examination of ideas, for it requires a distinctive kind of active immersion in the entire tradition of Jewish learning. Study of the Torah is most poignantly the means whereby Jews enter into the very process of creation and revelation. The Torah is understood to comprise within itself all the keys to reality since it is the mystical blueprint of the universe itself. The Torah is the absolute focus of meaning for Judaism, and all beliefs and practices are predicated on its acceptance.

In its major early sources Judaism has no word for 'religion' or 'spiritual'. This is because Judaism makes no such division between religious and non-religious spheres; it has no concept of non-spiritual, or material, things existing devoid of any ongoing reference to the divine. For Judaism, everything is part of one wholeness which is always, and everywhere, 'spiritual' in the sense of being an expression of the divine Will. This perspective ensues from Judaism's most fundamental belief, that of monotheism. In its central statement that God is One, Judaism implicitly understands that all reality is ultimately unified through its dependence on God. God in Himself, however, transcends all reality. As the rabbis put it, 'God is the place of the world, but the world is not His place'.

In Jewish belief, God is an active presence in the world as a whole and in the life of each individual. He did not simply create the world and withdraw to let it run by itself. The world is totally dependent on the continual creative power of God. As a *personal* God, He is engaged in all facets of an individual's life. In particular, He may respond to one's aspirations, as expressed, for example, in prayer. As the Talmud puts it, 'If a man will sanctify himself a little, God will sanctify him more and more'.[2] Judaism incorporates three formal prayer services each day, morning, afternoon and evening, with additional services on Shabbat and festivals. Spontaneous and private prayer have their place also, as do meditation and other mystical practices.

God totally transcends any image we may apply to Him. Hebrew literature, especially the Bible, employs anthropomorphic imagery – such as that of God's love or anger, or of His limbs – in order to express God's qualities in terms that humans can comprehend. But such terms are relative only and do not express the true nature of God. Even calling God 'He' is a product of human convention.

Orthodox Jewish belief holds that God has revealed Himself to humankind collectively through His 'descent' onto Mount Sinai, as recorded in the book of Exodus. The Torah is the lasting testimony of this revelation. The Torah is the Word of God as passed through the hand of Moses. As such it is the source of all wisdom, both as a guide to the nature of ultimate reality and as a code of conduct. The revelation included both the *written* and the *oral* Torah. The Oral Torah is the body of teachings whereby the correct understanding of the written text may be arrived at. Indeed, study of the Torah is largely concerned with the elucidation of the written text through the agency of the oral tradition. As indicated above, such study is understood to be the most sublime of all possible human endeavours. Non-Orthodox branches of Judaism may question both the literalness of the biblical image of revelation and the authority of the oral tradition, but generally share this sense of the Torah as embodying some form of higher truth.

History is seen as *purposeful* in the sense that it is itself an expression of God's Will. The history of the world in general, and of the Jewish people in particular, is directed towards the ultimate goal of salvation. Judaism holds that the intention which lay behind God's initial creation of the world will become manifest through a final age of peace and unification. This idea is expressed in the concept of the 'Messiah'. The Messiah has generally been viewed as a human figure to be sent by God, who will appear either when human conduct merits it, or towards the end of the world's allotted span of time. He will be the key figure in the restoration of full national and religious autonomy to the Jewish people. The days of the Messiah will be a time when earthly life will be infused with a clear vision of the Oneness of God and His purpose. In writings of the Reform movement in particular there is a tendency to discard the personalistic aspect of the Messiah whilst retaining the notion of a Messianic Age as a kind of final golden age to world history.

Such statements of the nature of God and of His purposes in the world are necessarily somewhat abstract. As mentioned above, Judaism is primarily oriented more towards actions than towards abstract statements of belief. Indeed, theology as such is somewhat foreign to traditional Jewish thought. Judaism is fundamentally directed towards *the refinement of human action*; it is more immediately a way of life than a set of beliefs. Jewish teaching, as focused in the Torah, indicates the ways in which human behaviour may be brought in line with the Will of God. Such are the ways of *holiness*. All walks of life are covered by this teaching, not only those that tend to be classed as 'religious' by today's outlook. As far as Judaism in daily life is concerned, belief in God is hardly an issue, for the way one acts is much more important than the kinds of beliefs one embraces.

RITUAL

For average Jews today, it is their active involvement in the ritual life of Judaism that cements their identity as Jews. The defining feature of Jewish identity is in fact established by birth, not by some declaration of faith. (The arduous path of conversion to Judaism effectively forges a mystical bond between the convert and the progenitors of the Jewish people, Abraham and Sarah.) Children born of a Jewish mother are Jewish, irrespective of their beliefs or practice later in life. The only exception is in the case of one who chooses to convert to an idolatrous religion, and whose Jewish status is thereby compromised. In today's world, in which assimilation of Jews into non-religious society is a major concern for Judaism, the legal question of status through birth is less pressing than the more psycho-social one of involvement in Judaism's ritual life. In our day, many Jews, whose status as Jews is not in question, have drifted away from the religion. However, 'non-religious' Jews may still identify themselves with aspects of Judaism's ritual life. This is largely because Judaism is in many ways a culture as well as a religion, and its ritual life, especially as it revolves around the family, is the primary root of its cultural integrity. It is particularly in relation to the historical experience of Jews as 'outsiders' that these issues of cultural, and sociological, identity have come about.

THE HOME

The ritual life of Judaism is strongly focused in the home, and the family unit is central to much religious activity. Festivals, for example, are celebrated around the meal table. The meal itself is not simply an adjunct to a festivity but often becomes the central vehicle for expressing the religious value of the day. The meal table becomes the equivalent in our day to the altar in the Temple of biblical times. It is the true centre of our interaction with God through ritual. Prayers configuring the holiness of the festive day are recited at the table; children are educated at the table; and words of Torah should be studied at the table. Preparing and eating the food itself are acts infused with holiness through awareness of the divine order of things. Moreover, the essential compassionate face of Judaism should be expressed by inviting guests to one's table.

The focus of the weekly Sabbath (*Shabbat*), for example, is as much on the three meals of the day, each of which is dedicated to a different aspect of the day's holiness, as it is on the prayers offered in the synagogue. Many features of the practice of Judaism are concerned with observance of Shabbat and the festivals of the religious calendar. Shabbat, as discussed in Chapter 3, is a day set aside from regular passing time as having a special holiness. It is marked by cessation of creative physical work. It is a day for prayer, song, and study. Each festival has its own specific practices according to the spiritual message it carries.

The clearest example of the centrality of the home comes with the spring festival of Passover (*Pesach*). As will be discussed more fully in Chapter 5, Pesach recollects the freedom from slavery brought about by the Exodus from Egypt. This event lies at the very heart of Judaism, and the festival is focused on the imperative of passing on its message. This is achieved primarily through the vehicle of the festive gathering – the *seder* meal – around the family table at the commencement of the festival. All participants, from the very young to the very old, are encouraged to question, discuss, and study – according to their ability – the Exodus and its meaning, both to the Jewish people as a whole and to themselves as individuals. It is particularly incumbent on parents to convey the lessons to their children. The festive meal itself comprises many symbolic foods which in their own way further the lessons of the Exodus. Bitter herbs, for example, evoke the bitterness of slavery. The primary symbol of Pesach, unleavened bread (*matzah*), not only reminds us of the speed with which we departed Egypt (Exodus 12:39), but also hints at the dangers of pride. Leaven (that is, food that has risen) becomes a symbol of the way in which pride 'puffs up' the ego, thereby holding one back from experiencing the true freedom to which the festival is directed. Beyond its reference to liberation from slavery, the freedom celebrated on Pesach refers to the concept of spiritual freedom, a state only

11

attained through sacrifice of the petty desires and delusions of one's ego.

The home is also the focus for other key elements of the practice of Judaism – its dietary laws and laws of family purity in particular. In brief, the many regulations surrounding diet stipulate the kinds of animals and fish that may be consumed, as well as the manner in which an animal should be killed. Orthodox practice maintains strict separation between meat and milk products. This entails not only refraining from eating one class of food for several hours following consumption of the other class, but also ensuring that utensils used for meat are separate from those used for milk products. These laws are understood to be immutable. Many discussions of the meaning of the dietary laws have been given, ranging from the medical to the mystical. But, as we shall see in more general terms in Chapter 4, the laws of the Torah are upheld primarily because they are understood to embody the Will of God. Discussion of their meanings is certainly important and serves to deepen one's spiritual awareness; but such discussion should not distract from the primacy of action and acceptance that the laws express a higher, if unknown, purpose.

Such attention to detail in matters of the home becomes most pronounced in the run up to Pesach. The whole house is subject to intense scrutiny to ensure that no leaven, or crumbs of old food, might be around. In effect, this entails a total spring clean and change of kitchen utensils. The arrival of the seder comes as a great climax following these preparations, and is followed by a period of seven days (eight days outside Israel) in which foods which have employed raising agents or have in any way involved fermentation are scrupulously avoided.

The role of the home is crucial as far as education is concerned. In its traditions, Judaism is acutely aware of the importance of education, both through study and through example. Many a Jewish person's earliest memories revolve around the ambience surrounding some religious festival in the home. Even be it only the smell of some food, for example, such a memory becomes bound together with the religious symbols, prayers, and words of teaching that accompanied it. The child's foundation in Judaism is often established in such a fashion.

WOMEN IN JUDAISM

The role of women in Judaism is traditionally related to this emphasis on the centrality of the home. A 'home' is not simply a place to which one may return to rest; it is the active focus of religious life and, as such, has to be created. In the family unit, the wife's spiritual fulfilment was traditionally achieved through such creativity. Of course, as society itself has changed so changes have developed in religious roles. Contemporary Judaism displays a spectrum of attitudes to female spirituality. Thus, Orthodox Judaism, whilst recognizing the importance of women's spiritual aspirations, considers that certain features of traditional roles in regard to Jewish practice are immutable. Reform Judaism, by comparison, largely sees women as able to fill any and all roles traditionally ascribed to men only. These differences are bound up with the respective traditions' approaches to deep spiritual principles and will be explored more fully in Chapter 7.

ISRAEL

Finally, I come to the place of Israel in Jewish consciousness. The equation of Zionism with what is generally understood as nationalism is very misleading, and has become the vehicle for a peculiarly modern form of anti-semitism. The Zionist ideal is not simply a political goal grafted onto a group of people defined by some cultural or social heritage. Jerusalem, to which the biblical word 'Zion' refers, and Israel itself occupy an absolutely central place within the corpus of Jewish teaching and tradition. 'By the rivers of Babylon, there we sat down, yea we wept, when we remembered Zion', cries the Psalmist (Psalm 137:1). Judaism without Jerusalem is a body without a heart. All prayers have focused on Zion for two thousand years; many commandments of the Torah can operate only in relation to the Land of Israel; Jewish history – which is seen as the vehicle of God's presence in the world – is ultimately defined in relation to Israel; and Jews have always aspired to settle in the Land of Israel when conditions permitted. The return to Israel is understood by most religious Jews within the context of the purpose of history as described above, and as a forerunner to the days of the Messiah.

This is not to deny that there are problems of a social and political nature which present huge challenges to the people and the leadership of the State of Israel. This book is not, however, the forum for discussion of such issues. To the extent that Judaism's claim on the Land of Israel is predicated on the historical experience of the Jewish people, the meaning of Israel is fundamentally religious, not political. This religious meaning of Israel – as an inner spiritual ideal and as a real State in the world – constitutes a key element of Judaism's belief system. Moreover, as far as practice is concerned, moving from the diaspora to live in Israel is recognized as a religious obligation, to be followed assuming circumstances allow it.

With few exceptions, Jews identify with Israel. They may argue over its political or cultural direction, or over the balance between secular and religious power. But, as the old saying has it, when two Jews are gathered you will always find three opinions! The existence of the State of Israel has infused a spirit of creative renewal into Judaism which extends throughout the diaspora. It has also introduced a unifying element. A challenge to which Jews throughout the world feel a special bond and responsibility, for example, is that of integrating Jews of diverse backgrounds into Israeli society. Jews from practically all parts of the world, including those whose societies had hardly been touched by the twentieth century, jostle in the streets of Jerusalem and Tel Aviv. Such a mixture of people itself provides the melting pot out of which creative renewal grows. Whether or not such creative expressions of the Jewish spirit are directly offered in the name of religion, they will undoubtedly influence the development of Judaism into the next century.

2 · TORAH: THE ESSENCE OF JUDAISM

It [Torah] is a tree of life to those who grasp it and those who sustain it are happy. Its ways are ways of pleasantness and all its paths are peace (Proverbs 3:18 & 17).

THE 'SEA OF TORAH'

To understand anything of Judaism it is necessary first of all to grasp its concept of the Torah. Torah is the essence of Judaism, and the whole of Judaism's long history may be viewed as one of exploring the meaning and ramifications of the Torah. To convey in a simple definition what is meant by the term, Torah, is impossible. Furthermore, whatever the Torah may be conceived to be from the outside will inevitably miss something of its true nature. For Torah is something that is *lived*. It is the Way, the very soul of the world. In the quotation from Proverbs above, which is also found in the prayer book, we are enjoined to *grasp* it. The word is not merely metaphorical – the ideal is that a kind of mystical union should take place with the Torah as a means to the most complete relationship with God. Such union leads to the realization that Torah is a form of transcendent wisdom; a higher reality whose essence cannot truly be captured by the words we use in relation to mundane reality. The Torah, then, is more than the book or scroll that constitutes its outer face, just as we are more than the flesh and blood that is our physical reality. For Judaism, the Torah is a vital presence, a 'mighty stream of living waters' in which our own souls are rooted.

In traditional rabbinic literature the phrase, the 'sea of Torah', is used. The image is powerful for several reasons. The sea is teeming with life and permanently in flux. Its waters form one unified whole. Similarly in the case of Torah: to the rabbinic mind, it is an indivisible, living presence. Thus, for example, in interpreting its words, widely separated phrases may be juxtaposed with no abnegation of logic. The words themselves penetrate into the deeper, seamless whole which is the real Torah. A second parallel views the sea's great power to affect the physical landscape in relation to the Torah's impact on the inner, spiritual and mental, landscape. Indeed, the parallel is not only to our inner make-up, for Torah is understood to be the very agent by means of which the world was created and continues to be maintained. Furthermore, water itself is the fount of life: 'As water gives life to the world,' says the Midrash,[1] 'so does the Torah give life to the world.' Finally, and perhaps most symbolically, the Torah may be compared to the sea because the sea reflects the heavens:

> R. Meir said: What distinguishes blue from all other colours? It is because blue resembles the sea, the sea resembles the firmament, and the firmament resembles the Throne of Glory, as it is written, '[They saw the God of Israel] and under His feet, as it were, a paved work of sapphire stones, and it was like the essence of heaven in clarity' (Exodus 24:10).[2]

Just as the sea is an earthly reflection of the heavenly Throne of Glory, so does Torah reflect the face of God on earth.

There can be no comprehension of what the Torah means to Judaism without recognizing these cosmic dimensions. Judaism conceives of the cosmos as built on correspondences between different levels of reality, as is hinted at in these words of R. Meir. Everything in our world – that is, the lower realm in the cosmic design – is dependent on the higher realm, Torah not only conveys an understanding of the higher world to us, but it is itself the very means through which this cosmic design exists. It is thus the central instrument of creation:

> R. Eliezer said: Great is Torah for were it not for the Torah heaven and earth could not endure, as it says, '[Thus says the Lord:] If my covenant had not [endured] day and night, then the laws of heaven and earth I would not have set' (Jeremiah 33:25).[3]

THE TORAH AS A BLUEPRINT

The Torah was given to humankind via an act which Judaism regards as unique – the revelation at Mount Sinai. This act was the high point of the Exodus from Egypt, the journey out from slavery. The many traditional stories concerning the events at Sinai at the time of this revelation convey the sense of urgency, as it were, about God's attempt to bring the Torah down to earth. The Midrash informs us that it was offered to various groups of people who, for one reason or another, rejected it. Finally the chance fell to the people of Israel. On one level, God was offering the chance of spiritual guidance. On another, however, the real issue was the survival of creation itself: 'God said to the works of creation: If Israel receive the Torah you will continue, but if not then I will return you to the state of form-lessness and void'.[4] In other words, without the agreement of a people to accept the Torah – that is to bring it firmly into the earthly realm – it could not have played its role in maintaining the cosmic design. Moreover, the whole purpose of creation could not be achieved without such an acceptance.

Torah is understood to play a variety of roles in the scheme of things. It is the blueprint which God used as a guide to creation itself. It is the agent which maintains creation. It is God's revelation to humankind. It is the guide for a spiritually and socially viable society. To see the relationship between these various roles is to glimpse something of the 'real' Torah which is beyond the divisions of space and time. It is certainly not simply a book of rules. It is perhaps best described as the means by which the essence of God's thought becomes manifest through human endeavour. Our actions are to be directed by Torah and our minds should be enlightened by study of Torah. In this way the heavenly and earthly realms are brought into harmonious relationship.

The dictionary definition of Torah is 'the five books of Moses'. However, I hope it is clear already that this is inadequate. How could mere books be of such ultimate value? Torah refers to the whole of God's revelation. The immediate focus of such revelation is indeed the 'five books', but in rabbinic literature Torah includes all revelation, as manifest both before and after the historical event at Mount Sinai. The creation itself is part of God's revelation and is, accordingly, a manifestation of the Torah:

> 'In the beginning God created' (Genesis 1:1). R. Hoshaya commenced thus: 'Then I was beside Him as an 'amon and I was His delight day by day' (Proverbs 8:30) . . . 'Amon is a craftsman ('uman). The Torah says: 'I was the design implement of the Holy One, blessed be He'. This may be compared with a king of flesh and blood who builds a palace not on the basis of his own knowledge but on that of an architect. And further, the architect does not rely on his current knowledge alone, but uses plans and diagrams to discern where to make rooms and gates. Thus the Holy One, blessed be He, gazed into the Torah and created the world. Indeed, the Torah says, 'By means of a beginning God created' and there is no beginning other than Torah, as it says, 'The Lord acquired me as the beginning of His way' (Proverbs 8:22). ['me' in this verse refers to Wisdom, alluding to the Torah.][5]

This is one of many sayings in which the pre-existence of Torah and its key role in creation are discussed. It is worth emphasizing here the way in which central ideas are built from subtleties discerned in the original scriptural passages. This is a major exegetical technique. Many interpretations arise through analysis of the Hebrew of the Bible. Such analysis is rooted in a feeling for the holiness of the language itself, as well as in a sense that the language of biblical texts is able to reveal greater truth than that given by the surface meaning alone. The nature of biblical Hebrew enables a kind of creative word-play which became a support to the kinds of insights the rabbis wished to convey. In particular, the fact that the Hebrew of sacred texts consists only of consonants introduces a certain fluidity into their reading. The absence of vowels means that a given word can have a variety of possible pronunciations, and therefore meanings. Although the 'correct' pronunciation and meaning are known from the oral tradition, it is understood that other possible meanings, including those of related words, may bear on the passage's deeper significance.

In relation to the quoted passage, the Hebrew root 'amn connotes 'faithfulness' (note the connection with 'amen'), 'teaching', and 'nurturing' as well as coming to mean a 'craftsman' or 'architect'. The role of Torah as a pre-existent guide to creation as well as its continuing function as the guide to human spiritual endeavour is captured better by this cluster of meanings than by any single word. The last point in the quotation, concerning the opening phrase in Genesis, plays on the ambiguity in the initial letter *bet*. Whilst this letter could give the meaning 'in', as 'In the beginning', it can also mean 'with' or 'by means of'. Hence, the rabbis point to the concept being 'By means of a beginning . . .', and derive the idea that Torah was the agent, existing prior to the opening sentence of Genesis, by means of which God brought about creation.

THE TORAH AS REVELATION

Regarding manifestations of God's revelation seemingly after Sinai, the term Torah has an extended sense whereby it includes all inspirational works, which, in one way or another, draw out the meaning or implications of the original five books:

> When God was about to give the Torah, He recited it to Moses in order: Bible, Mishnah, Aggadah, and Talmud, for it says 'And God spoke *all* these words' (Exodus 20:1), even the answers to questions which learned wise men will ask their teachers in the future did God reveal to Moses, for He spoke *all* these words.[6]

Since Judaism understands that God Himself is the author of the Torah, it is axiomatic that every single word and letter is present for a purpose, whether or not we can discern the meaning in a simple sense. The rabbis therefore attempted to attach meanings to words which might be construed as superfluous to the straightforward sense of the text. Thus, in the quotation above, the word 'all' becomes the key to this conception of the extension of Torah into all its authentic interpretations and elaborations. For the word 'all' would not be necessary if the only intention of the text were to suggest that God spoke all the words which followed (namely the ten commandments) – it would have been obvious. The word 'all' becomes available for a deeper meaning, namely that the words spoken included all their commentaries. Such exegesis of the text of the Torah lies at the heart of rabbinic Judaism. As the Talmud puts it, 'Just as a plant grows and increases, so the words of Torah grow and increase'.[7]

The Hebrew word, 'Torah', itself derives from the root, yrh, meaning 'to shoot' (an arrow). A second meaning of this root is 'to teach'. Torah is the teaching; that which directs individuals beyond their immediate horizons, like the arrow arching into the distance. In its fullest sense, Torah is that which attaches the individual to the inner workings of creation, for, as indicated above, it is the very agent by means of which God creates the world. Furthermore, since it is the ultimate blueprint of creation there is nothing which may not be found within it:

> Ben Bag-Bag says, turn it [Torah] around, turn it around, for all is in it. Meditate in it and grow old and grey over it. Stir not from it, for there is no quality better than it.[8]

Such a statement does not simply designate a book which happens to be exceptionally profound. The quality of Torah lies in its transcendent nature. Judaism holds Torah to be a window into the infinite. By meditating within it, the individual aspires to the deepest mysteries which somehow embrace all shades of the reality we live in. This is the 'all' to which Ben Bag-Bag refers.

The name of this sage perhaps deserves a slight digression. It is almost as comical in Hebrew as it is in English! Furthermore, the aphorism which follows ('According to the effort is the reward') is quoted in the name of Ben Heh-Heh which also has a strange ring to it. It is generally accepted that these are fictitious names and that in making them up emphasis was placed on the numerical value of the Hebrew letters (gematria). 'Bag' has the value of five which is the numerical value of the fifth Hebrew letter, *heh*. There is thus some equivalence between the two names. The emphasis on five conveys the centrality of this number to Torah (*five* books). *Bg-Bg* is essentially five repeated – ten, and brings to mind the description of the covenant in the *Sefer Yetzirah*, an early mystical work, as witnessed by the ten fingers, 'five opposite five'. Raising the two hands with outstretched fingers symbolizes acceptance of the Torah and the furtherance of its role in uniting heaven and earth through the intermediary of human consciousness. Exploring its ramifications, as advised by Ben Bag-Bag, is central to this profound role which Torah plays in the scheme of things.

There is no containing the meaning of Torah in a package that sits comfortably within the rational mind. The mystery of the origin and nature of Torah is the *sine qua non* of religious belief. If there were no mystery, all the aspects of Judaism to be presented in the following pages would be merely human in scale. The rituals, prayers and laws are branches which all draw their spiritual sustenance from the one root they share in common – the Torah.

THE MYSTERY OF THE TORAH

The major work of Jewish mysticism, The *Zohar*, explains that the Torah is much more than the stories it contains. Were the stories the important content, then we might imagine there could be better, even more meaningful, stories. No, the stories are only a surface and point the way to the real Torah, the 'Torah of Truth'. One must enter into the depths of the Torah to find such truth. An image employed in this context is that of a beautiful woman, hidden in her palace, who yearns for her lover. Like the woman, the real Torah may not be found from a passing look. She may reveal her face fleetingly but only to entice her lover further. He must actively search her out. The ultimate relationship is achieved by the person who delves deeply into the mysteries of the Torah. It becomes a relationship between that person's soul and the inner essence of Torah – an encounter not with words or letters but with the very process of God's thought.

The central tenet of Judaism is that the Torah is *min ha-shamayim*, 'from heaven'. The mystery of Torah is the same mystery as that inherent in God's descent to Mount Sinai: 'He bent the higher and lower heavens down and spread them on the top of the mountain . . . and the Throne of Glory descended upon them', comments Rashi, the authoritative voice on the meaning of the scriptural text. This comment is provided to reconcile an apparent contradiction between two verses in Exodus concerning the revelation at Mount Sinai. Exodus 19:20 states: 'And the Lord descended upon Mount Sinai to the top of the mountain'. According to Exodus 20:19, however, God says that, 'You have seen that from heaven I spoke with you'. So where was He – in heaven or on earth at the top of the mountain? The answer given as above is *both*. It was not that God came from heaven to the mountain; Sinai became heaven and earth combined. The mystery of the revelation at Sinai concerns the interpenetration of heaven and earth. For Judaism, the subtlety of the relationship between transcendence and immanence underlies these concrete images of God's revelation of the Torah on the mountain. Torah is the very embodiment of the transcendent realm in an immanent, or accessible, form.

Mountains are often imbued with sacred significance. Mountains soar to the heights and easily inspire awe. But Judaism conveys an important second idea here. Sinai is not the highest mountain in the region. The Midrash tells us that it was chosen for this great event on account of its 'humility'. This is to teach that, in a parallel sense, humility is a necessary condition for the individual to be worthy to receive Torah. Such was Moses' character and such is the ideal for all. Indeed, much play is made of the significance of the revelation being in the desert:

'He who makes himself as a desert, the Torah is given to him as a gift', says the Talmud. In contemporary language, overcoming one's ego, or freeing oneself from the strings built up through conditioning, is the prerequisite to the 'higher state' which Torah represents.

The Talmud conveys the point by means of some penetrating analysis of Hebrew double meanings in a few verses from the book of Numbers (21:17–20). It is perhaps worth dwelling on this passage to give a flavour of the manner in which subtle meanings and hints may be discerned under the surface of the Torah's narrative. The scriptural text runs:

> Then Israel sang this song:
>   'Spring up, O well; Sing unto it.
>   A well the princes [Moses and Aaron] dug;
>   the nobles of the people hewed it out,
>   by the direction of the law–giver, with their staves.'
> And from the desert they went to Matanah. And from Matanah to Nahaliel, and from Nahaliel to Bamot. And from Bamot to the valley that is in the field of Moab.

On the surface we have here a fragment from the history of the various journeyings of the Children of Israel through the desert. In a deeper sense the words concern the Torah and the states an individual passes through in acquiring it. The poignancy of these few words is intimated by the first word, 'then', which in Hebrew is *'az*. The two Hebrew letters in this word, *'alef* and *zayin* are the first and seventh letters of the alphabet. The *alef* symbolizes the transcendent source (see appendix) whilst the *zayin* represents the world of experience, our world characterized as it is by cycles (seven being the glyph of cyclical time). A translation can only ever convey the outer, literal meaning. The English 'then' implies a static historical event, but the Hebrew *'az* has a deeper connotation, denoting an ever-present state of potential. It refers to a state in which a spiritually higher level is accessed. The timeless source of the spiritual dimension (*'alef*) has been glimpsed from within the space-time framework of our immediate reality (*zayin*). The *Bahir*, an influential early kabbalistic work, connects this word with the raising of hands towards heaven, again intimating a state whereby a higher realm is accessed. Indeed, the number eight (that is, *'alaf* plus *zayin*) is specifically related to the Torah by R. Judah Leow, the Maharal of Prague, because it transcends the natural world. A parallel may be drawn with the musical scale in which the eighth note is a recapitulation of the first at a higher level.

The first line in the quoted passage is a reference to the 'Song of the Sea' which Moses and the Children of Israel sang when they came through the Sea of Reeds to escape the Egyptians. In Chapter 5, the spiritual meaning of the Exodus story will be examined in some depth. As will be explained, passing through the sea on dry land depicts the progression from one realm of existence to a higher, more spiritual one. Thus, the reference is deliberate and designed to indicate how the scriptural passage under consideration is also concerned with the relationship between a lower sphere and a higher one.

In our passage the song is about a well. The symbolism is quite direct. The well connects to a source; it is a point of access to the life-giving waters. In Hebrew *be'ar*, a 'well', is an anagram of *bara'*, 'to create'. Just as the act of creation depends upon an influx of potential from a higher sphere, so too the well is a point of access to that higher sphere. (Of course, 'lower' and 'higher' have no spatial connotation here; the source of water, deep underground, depicts a 'higher' level in spiritual terms.) The well symbolizes a two-way process: the water only becomes available through the endeavour involved in digging the well in the first place. Here again, the image is powerful in relation to the Torah. As quoted above, 'According to the effort is the reward'. As one delves into a scriptural passage so one may merit the receipt of some insight. This two-way process is very much of the essence of Torah.

THE MEANING OF WORDS

The talmudic text itself focuses on the names of places mentioned in the latter part of the passage. It is central to the notion of Torah as comprising hidden levels of meaning that, on deeper inspection, names yield particular significance and are not arbitrary. The text, quoted in the name of R. Yosef bar Hama, runs as follows:

> If a man makes himself like this desert on which all trample, then Torah is given to him as a gift [Hebrew word *matanah* means a gift]. And if it is given to him as a gift, God makes it an inheritance, as it says, 'And from Matanah to Nahaliel [the word *nahali'el* means inheritance of God].' If God makes it an inheritance, then he rises to greatness, as it says, 'And from Nahaliel to Bamot [*bamot* means heights].' But if he allows his heart to swell with pride, the Holy One, blessed be He, humbles him, as it says, 'And from Bamot to the valley.' If he returns, however, the Holy One, blessed be He, lifts him up, as it says, 'Every valley shall be uplifted' (Isaiah 40:4).[9]

The process of acquiring Torah through study is the spiritual ascent itself, and we have in this talmudic passage a clear depiction of its stages and pitfalls. The story of the Children of Israel and their wanderings is the same story as that of all individuals in their quest for the 'promised land'. Without humility in the first place, the individual will not be open to the spark of the divine fire which lies in their own soul and in the Torah. As the individual labours in Torah, so it becomes not only a gift but an inheritance, a part of their self. It is a presence which connects with all the generations in a continuous line to Sinai. Indeed, it is said that all souls were present at the revelation. We each have a portion in Torah, and our spiritual quest is directed to becoming conscious of that hidden part of ourselves which knows where its source of nourishment lies.

As individuals grow in their spiritual life, so the danger of pride reappears. Knowledge brings power in its wake, and power, as the saying goes, corrupts. In a psychological sense, the process of delving through the levels of Torah is akin to delving deeper into oneself. Advance in the spiritual path brings a deeper insight into events and people around one. Of course, things are not so simple as this sounds. The path laid out in Judaism involves much beyond study alone – as we will consider in future chapters. But as far as study itself is concerned, great emphasis is laid on the dangers of pride.

Judaism stresses that study of Torah must be *lishmah*, 'for its own sake'. One studies not for personal gain, but because such study is enjoined on one – 'it is for this that you were created'. A forceful warning is given by R. Banah in a play on the word *sam* which has the double meaning of 'elixir' and 'poison':

> R. Banah says: 'Anyone who studies Torah *lishmah*, his Torah becomes for him an elixir of life, as it says, 'It is a tree of life to them that grasp it' (Proverbs 3:18); 'It shall be health to your navel' (Proverbs 3:8); and 'For whosoever finds Me finds life' (Proverbs 8:35). But anyone who studies Torah not *lishmah*, it becomes for him a poison of death, as it says, 'My doctrine shall drip like the rain' (Deuteronomy 32:2), and there is no dripping ['*arefah*] other than killing, as it says, 'They shall decapitate [same root as '*arefah*] the calf in the valley' (Deuteronomy 21:4). [10]

It should be clear that Torah study cannot be equated with the normal, intellectual act of study. Indeed, the Hebrew word for Torah study, '*asaq*, has the connotation of being immersed in, and of effecting a transaction. Torah study is distinguished as embracing the whole person. Even God Himself is said to study Torah each day, which perhaps conveys something of the cosmic significance attached to Torah study. Study without practice is, however, futile, for then it degenerates into an intellectual act alone. As well as being a blueprint for creation, the Torah is a blueprint for one's conduct, both in an ethical sense and in terms of religiously prescribed behaviour (*mitzvot*). Study is the vital underpinning to such 'right conduct'. Study not only brings familiarity with the rules themselves but also enables the ramifications of those rules to be discerned in everyday life.

THE STUDY OF TORAH

Torah study becomes a parallel to the process of creation itself. In Jewish thinking, creation is characterized by, first, establishing principles or generalities, and only secondly by drawing out the particularities. In the Genesis story, for example, it is the principle of light which is created first (day 1) and only subsequently (day 4) are the particular bodies which emit light created. The point here is that Torah study, which draws out the particularities of the text in terms of both intellectual and practical meaning, is the paradigm of creation itself. Torah is a spark of heaven, but it is only through study that it is truly brought down to earth. Study completes the circuit between heaven and earth, which was the initial aim of creation. It is difficult to find the right word to convey exactly what Judaism understands by Torah study. The aim is one of *actualizing* the Torah; bringing it into the reality of our world. God revealed His Torah but it is the responsibility of humankind to bring it to life, as it were. Judaism sees humankind as very much the partner to God in furthering, and ultimately fulfilling, the aims of creation. Torah is the indispensable cement to this partnership.

The Torah itself offers a cryptic hint to the idea that study and exposition of the text is an absolutely central pursuit. The word at the exact middle of the Torah, in terms of the total number of words, is *darash* (Leviticus 10:16). Moreover, the word is doubled (*darosh darash*), which is the Hebrew means of conveying emphasis. The verb *darash* means to investigate or expound. It is the root of the Hebrew, *Midrash*, which refers to the body of rabbinic expositions on the homiletic meaning of Torah. *Darosh darash* at the centre of the Torah intimates that study is not simply a useful addition – as would be the case with a secular work. Without study the Torah becomes devoid of its very heart.

The techniques employed in the study of Torah are contingent on an attitude of absolute respect for the scriptural text. Commentators may emphasize the significance of a single letter, its numerical value, its position in a word, its transposition into another letter by some cryptic code, for example. To a modern, rational mind these approaches are bizarre in the extreme. Any insights gleaned through such devices are surely not of the essence of the text – so the sceptic may argue – they could not have been planted into the text in its origin.

But, answers the Orthodox Jewish mind, that origin is divine. By definition, all worlds of meaning are inherent in the Torah. In some kabbalistic writings, the Torah is even explicitly identified with God. Thus the thirteenth-century Italian kabbalist, Recanati, writes: 'God is nothing outside from the Torah, neither is the Torah something outside God'.[11] This identification of Torah with God becomes the keynote in the mystical quest for union with the divine. Penetrating the mysteries of Torah is in itself the means of such union. The act of exploring the fluidity in its text through the permutations of Hebrew letters, words and ideas, opens the mysterious link to the infinite in the mystic's own soul.

Figure 1 presents a schematization of the role of Torah study in Judaism. At the same time as depicting the scope of Torah study, it conveys something of the history of Judaism. Whilst political, cultural and social factors have all undoubtedly helped shape the Jewish way of life, Torah is the essence of Judaism. From the orthodox religious vantage point, Judaism exists to maintain the presence of Torah in the world, and this is achieved only through study. Moreover, different historical ages demand different aspects of the revelation to be brought to the fore. Thus, in one age, the Talmud, with its emphasis on legalistic issues, was the appropriate vehicle for the further-ance of Torah study. In another age, it was the *Zohar*, with its emphasis on mysticism. What is generally regarded as normal thinking is somewhat stood on its head by the authentic Jewish outlook, holding as it does that environmental factors fall into place around the central imperative – Torah study. In other words, successive stages in the actualization of Torah form the backbone around which other aspects of the history of Judaism – social, political and cultural – revolve.

At the centre of the figure is the Written Torah, so called because it is held that the written text itself was revealed from God. Surrounding this is the Oral Torah. Although the major works of the Oral Torah came to be written down (e.g., the Talmud), the term is used to emphasize the unbroken line of tradition from Moses himself, whereby the ideas contained in these works were transmitted.[12]

As we have seen, study proceeds in two complementary directions. On the one hand, the aim is a general, intellectual elucidation of the meaning of the text, and on the other hand, study is driven by the need to clarify the actual demands of

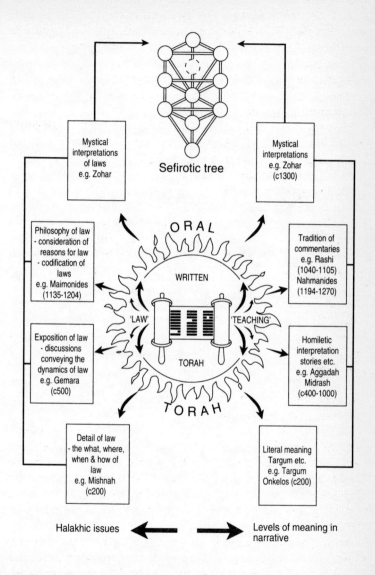

Sefirotic tree

Mystical
interpretations
of laws
e.g. Zohar

Mystical
interpretations
e.g. Zohar
(c1300)

ORAL

WRITTEN

Philosophy of law
- consideration of
reasons for law
- codification of
laws
e.g. Maimonides
(1135-1204)

Tradition of
commentaries
e.g. Rashi
(1040-1105)
Nahmanides
(1194-1270)

'LAW'   'TEACHING'

Exposition of law
- discussions
conveying the
dynamics of law
e.g. Gemara
(c500)

Homiletic
interpretation
stories etc.
e.g. Aggadah
Midrash
(c400-1000)

TORAH

TORAH

Detail of law
- the what, where,
when & how of
law
e.g. Mishnah
(c200)

Literal meaning
Targum etc.
e.g. Targum
Onkelos (c200)

Halakhic issues ◀━━━━▶ Levels of meaning in
narrative

Figure 1.   The scope of Torah and its study

29

the text in practice. Practical considerations are referred to as 'Halakhah', the subject of Chapter 4. Although it is helpful to separate these two aspects of Torah study, they inevitably interrelate. Understanding the subtleties in the scriptural text is generally essential in order that the halakhic issues may be fully drawn out. When it comes to the mystical level, this interrelationship obtains in a deeper sense. Jewish mystics see the Torah as a guide to the workings of a concealed world of 'sefirot', or divine emanations. The mystic penetrates the levels of meaning in Torah in order to arrive at the core which pertains to the nature of these sefirot. At the same time, actions prescribed by Halakhah are understood to promote the harmonious workings of the sefirotic world. In this way, mind (study) and body (actions) become united through the world of the sefirot.

SYMBOLIC LANGUAGE OF THE TORAH

I shall close this chapter with an example of the way in which subtle hints in a scriptural text can convey deeper meanings. In general, the deeper meanings of the Torah bear a kind of psycho-spiritual relevance which readily translates into modern language. Indeed, part of the work of Torah study is to effect a connection between the eternal language of Torah and the language, or cultural outlook, of one's own day.

Genesis 2 opens with the completion of the description of the first seven days of creation. Then comes the following cryptic sentence:

> These are the generations of the heaven and the earth when they were created, in the day that the Lord God made earth and heaven (Genesis 2:4).

There follows the so-called second creation story (which is really the second phase of what is one story) with its emphasis on the garden of Eden and the formation of woman.

The approach to study should always begin with questions. There are indeed many that may be asked of this verse, but I will cite only two. Why does the sequence heaven – earth change from the beginning to the end of the verse, and why the change from the verb 'create' to 'make'?

The answer to these questions lies in the observation that the text deliberately switches from an initial male-oriented description of creation to a subsequent female-oriented one. In Jewish thinking there are two impulses at work in creation – the impulse from above and the impulse from below, symbolized by male and female respectively. The emphasis of the second phase of the creation story is on the latter. Thus we read two verses further on that 'a mist (*'aid*) went up from the earth and watered the whole face of the ground'. The Hebrew *'aid*, is composed of the first two letters of the word *'adam*, 'humankind'. The mist is the creative impulse from 'mother' earth. *'Adam* combines these two letters with a third, the letter *mem* which symbolizes water. The mist first ascends and then descends to 'water' the ground. This whole cycle is intimated in the Hebrew name *'Adam*. It is not simply H_2O which is being discussed here; the deeper subject is the spiritual nature of humankind and the way in which we carry earth and heaven within us. Hence it is only now, in this second phase, that the *neshamah*, 'the soul', is introduced (Genesis 2:7). Indeed the soul is feminine, both in the grammatical sense of the word being feminine and also in the sense that it is symbolized by the letter *heh*, a letter intimating the feminine (see appendix).

This second phase of the creation story may be contrasted with the first in which each stage of creation is conveyed as a 'saying' of God. 'Let there be . . .' is the biblical way of expressing the active male orientation. It conveys the notion of creation *ex nihilo*. Genesis 1 depicts the initial dynamism of the creative imperative and its development through discrete stages ('days'). Its focus is the concrete nature of things, their outer form, whereas the second phase turns more towards inner qualities and potential.

Now, the verse I quoted is very much the pivotal point between the two phases and contains a further interesting feature. The phrase 'when they were created' is, in Hebrew, *be-hibar'am*. This word is an anagram of the Hebrew name *'Avraham* (Abraham). The Midrash, accordingly, comments on this verse by stating that heaven and earth were created 'in the merit of Abraham'. In the word *be-hibar'am* the letter *heh* is written deliberately small in the Torah scroll, which is a means of drawing attention to it. Later, in the story of Abraham, God changes his name from its original form of Abram by the addition of the letter *heh* (Genesis 17:5). That story itself is complex and conveys many issues which would take us too far afield. However, in essence, the story concerns a person becoming whole. For a man to reach his full potential he must acknowledge the female side of himself (as indeed must the woman acknowledge her male side). Hence the female letter *heh* is added to Abram's name.

The cryptic reference to Abraham in the verse quoted linking the two phases of the creation story serves to emphasize the human role in integrating the two aspects of creation, namely the outer and inner, or male and female. In a psychological sense this is the union of opposites to which Carl Jung refers in his analysis of the spiritual aspirations of the human psyche. The creation story is not simply a literal description of the beginnings of the physical universe. It becomes, more incisively, a depiction of the human condition – not only where we fit into the scheme of things but also our spiritual role in balancing the forces at work in the ongoing process of creation.

Every age generates its particular approach to the central issues of religion. In our day the kind of psycho-spiritual framework I have used in the foregoing paragraphs seems to be appropriate. The power of Torah lies in its ability to transcend the ephemeral fashions of language and ideas. It is precisely because the kinds of insight I have touched upon above are only hinted at in the text that every age can interpret them anew. This, then, gives us a central image of the place of Torah in Judaism. It is indeed a tree, rooted in Sinai, the trunk reaching up through thousands of years. The study of Torah gives rise to branches which key its teaching into the language and aspirations of the particular era. Thus is it 'a tree of life to those who grasp it'.

3 · SHABBAT AND TEMPLE

Shabbat (the Sabbath) is a central idea which Judaism has contributed to western society. That the work ethic should be tempered by the inclusion of at least one day of rest may in itself be viewed as somewhat liberating. But, as with many Jewish concepts, the superficial reading of its meaning fails to capture the special place which Shabbat occupies within the Jewish approach to spirituality. My juxtaposition of Shabbat with the Temple in this chapter reflects the rabbinic perspective on these matters and, in itself, introduces us to the spiritual dimension inherent in both.

In fact, the juxtaposition goes back to the Torah itself. The second half of the book of Exodus is devoted to a description of the *Mishkan*. The English translation of this word, 'tabernacle', is somewhat archaic and hardly serves to convey a clear meaning, so I shall use the Hebrew. 'Mishkan' derives from a root meaning 'to dwell'. It was the focus of spiritual life which enabled God's presence to dwell amongst the Children of Israel in the wilderness, and it became the pattern on which the Temple in Jerusalem was later built. The Mishkan was the transportable tent of meeting between God and the Children of Israel.

In the Torah, the connection between the Mishkan and Shabbat is intimated more than once. Following a preliminary description of the details of the Mishkan, a summary is given in Exodus 31:1–11. Immediately afterwards, one of

33

the major references to Shabbat is given (Exodus 31:12–17). Similarly, another reference to Shabbat, in Exodus 35:1–3, comes immediately prior to the description of the actual making of the Mishkan. Furthermore, twice in the book of Leviticus (19:30 and 26:2) we find an explicit pairing: 'My Shabbatot (Sabbaths) you shall keep and my Temple you shall revere. I am the Lord'.

These juxtapositions imply that there is a fundamental relationship between what the Mishkan (or the Temple) and Shabbat represent. Essentially, the relationship comes about since they both represent a special spiritual potency. Whilst, of course, there is no place or time which is inappropriate to spiritual endeavour, both Shabbat and the Mishkan offer a clearer focus to such endeavour. Shabbat offers a spiritual focus in *time*; the Mishkan offers a spiritual focus in *space*.

This relationship is further built upon in the Talmud and other rabbinic works. Thus, in establishing the laws applying to the practical observance of Shabbat, the rabbis deliberately invoked the categories of work which were employed in the building of the Mishkan:

> The categories of work prohibited on Shabbat are forty minus one. To what do they relate? R. Hanina bar Hama said to them, to the forms of labour used in constructing the Mishkan.[1]

The holiness of Shabbat is thus implicitly predicated on the holiness of the Mishkan. By refraining specifically from these categories of work, one establishes connection to the spiritual principles embodied in the Mishkan. Ideally, Shabbat becomes a 'temple in time', as the twentieth-century philosopher, Abraham Heschel, has called it.

In a more general sense the relationship between Shabbat and Temple focuses on the nature of creation itself. Both Shabbat and the Temple contain within themselves the whole of creation. As the crown of creation, Shabbat becomes a stage of reflection in which the whole may be grasped. Similarly, creating a temple, which is a sacred space, is a recapitulation of the original creation in which the ultimate sacred space – heaven and earth itself – was established. Thus Bezalel, the inspired builder of the Mishkan, was said to possess the secret of 'permuting the letters by which heaven and earth were created'.[2] Temple building and world building are two faces of the same inner imperative.

In midrashic sources we find the Temple depicted as the centre of the world, and as the point from which God builds the world. The 'foundation stone' of the whole earth becomes the base of the Holy of Holies, the spiritual centre of the Temple. This foundation stone was believed to have been the first object created and became the 'navel of the world' around which the world was constructed. In the Temple it becomes the rock on which the Holy Ark (see below) was placed.

A mediaeval Midrash, the *Pesikta Rabbati*, discerns an allusion to the relationship between Shabbat and the Temple in the language used in the initial description of Shabbat in Genesis, and that used to describe the completion of the Temple by King Solomon:

> 'And all the work of the House of the Lord was completed' (1 Kings 7:51). Not simply 'the work' but '*all* the work' is written – that is, on the day that the work of the Temple was finished, God declared that the work of the six days of creation was completed. Thus it is written, 'He rested from all His work which God created to make' (Genesis 2:3). 'Created and made' is not written but rather 'created *to make*', for there was still one work to do. When Solomon appeared and built the Temple, the Holy One, blessed be He, said, 'Now the work of heaven and earth is concluded and all the labour of creation is completed'. It is for this reason that he is called Solomon which means *complete* [Hebrew root *Shlm* = complete], because it was through the work of his hands that the Holy One, blessed be He, completed the work of the six days of creation.[3]

This quotation from *Pesikta Rabbati* suggests a further dimension of the relationship between Shabbat and the Mishkan/Temple. The quotation draws on the peculiar phrasing of Genesis 2:3. If the meaning was simply that God rested from his labours, surely the sentence should read that God rested from all His work which He had 'created and made'. But, as the quotation makes clear, the last verb is in the infinitive, as if to suggest that God created heaven and earth during the first six days but something was left over which was still to be made, or finalized.

This phrasing in Genesis has been the subject of much commentary. Essentially, the agreed implication is that some kind of window of opportunity was left open. In fact, the verse under consideration here comes immediately before the verse I discussed at the end of the last chapter:

> And God blessed the seventh day and made it holy, because in it He had rested from all His work which God created to make.
>
> These are the generations of the heaven and the earth when they were created. . . .

In the last chapter we saw how the latter verse includes a cryptic reference to Abraham as the paradigm of humanity's role in furthering the goals of creation. Both in himself and through his descendants, Abraham becomes the person who successfully grasps that window of opportunity. He recognizes the One God and brings the ideals of Torah to the world. Shabbat symbolizes the partnership between God and humanity. God gives of Himself in creation and we receive His presence by rising above the realm of purely physical existence, a rise in state represented by the holiness of Shabbat.

It is this reciprocal relationship which also lies at the heart of the Temple service. Although prayer and meditation have supplanted the role of animal sacrifice as practised in the Temple of Jerusalem, the underlying goal remains the same. The Hebrew for sacrifice, *korban*, derives from a root meaning 'to draw near'. The intention of sacrifice, or, more relevantly today, of prayer, is to effect a bridge between the lower and higher worlds in the cosmic plan. The prayer is a vehicle for the 'impulse from below' which draws forth the descent of a higher influx from above.

THE MISHKAN AND ITS CORRESPONDENCES

It is only in relation to the complex symbolism of the Mishkan, or Temple, that such ideas may be understood. In themselves they dissolve into superstition. The Mishkan/Temple represents the ideal place for such service because in its very structure it is held to resonate with the properties of the higher world. It is a microcosm of the totality of creation, as we shall shortly consider, and represents the penetration of the higher world into the finite lower world. Whilst the Torah is the fundamental principle allowing for the integration of higher and lower realms, the Temple is the place, and Shabbat is the time, wherein the potential for such integration is particularly concentrated.

The concept of the Temple as microcosm also keys it in to the archetypal nature of the human form, since this too is regarded as a microcosm ('In the image of God created He him'). Thus we have a three-way relationship – the macrocosm, or universe in its entirety, the Temple, and the human form. As expressed in the Midrash: 'The Temple corresponds to the whole world [macrocosm] and to the creation of man who is a small world [microcosm]'.[4]

There are numerous ways in which these relationships are drawn out. First, in the Torah itself there are many hints. One example of such a hint may be found in Exodus 39 where the completion of the Mishkan is described:

> And all the work of the Mishkan, the tent of meeting, was completed. And the Children of Israel made [it] according to all which the Lord had commanded Moses; thus they made [it]. And they brought the Mishkan to Moses, the tent and all its furnishings . . . (Exodus 39:32–3').[5]

There follows a complete list of all 'its furnishings'. The list includes thirty-two items (counted according to the Hebrew participle 'et). This number symbolically relates the Mishkan to both the macrocosm and the human body as microcosm. As far as the macrocosm is concerned, it is said that God created the universe with 'Thirty-two mystical paths of wisdom'.[6] And regarding the microcosm, thirty-two is the gematria of *lev*, 'heart', the centre of the body. Moreover, the heart is traditionally a focus for meditations designed to create one's own sacred space – a temple within. 'Everyone should build for himself a temple in the chambers of his heart', writes the nineteenth-century Malbim, 'For he should prepare himself to be a temple to God and a dwelling for the presence of His strength'.

The triple correspondence of Temple, universe or macro-cosm, and human form, is drawn out extensively through post-biblical writings, as in the following midrashic example:

> In the hour when the Holy One, blessed be He, said to Moses, Make me a Temple, Moses said, How shall I know how to make it? The Holy One, blessed be He, said, Do not get frightened; just as I created the world and your body, even so will you make the Mishkan. How [do we know] that this was so? You find in the Mishkan that the beams were fixed into sockets, and in the body the ribs are fixed into the vertebra, and so in the world the mountains are fixed into the fundaments of the earth. In the Mishkan the beams were covered with gold, and in the body the ribs are covered with flesh, and in the world the mountains are covered and coated with earth. In the Mishkan there were bolts in the beams to keep them upright, and in the body limbs and sinews are drawn to keep man upright, and in the world trees and grasses are drawn in the earth. In the Mishkan there were hangings to cover its top and both its sides, and in the body the skin of man covers his limbs and his ribs on both sides, and in the world the heavens cover the earth on both its sides. In the Mishkan the veil divided between the Holy Place and the Holy of Holies, and in the body the diaphragm divides the heart from the stomach, and in the world it is the firmament which divides between the upper waters and the lower waters.[7]

Elsewhere in early sources we find specific correspondences based upon the general layout of the Mishkan and its furniture. As can be seen in Figure 2, the Mishkan consisted of three areas: the outer court, the Holy Place and the Holy of Holies, which was separated from the Holy Place by a veil. The major furnishings included the Holy Ark in which were housed the tablets of stone given by God to Moses; the table on which was displayed the shewbread; the menorah – a golden lampstand; a golden altar for incense; a bronze altar for sacrifices; and a water basin for ritual purification.

Amongst the correspondences, we find the layout of the Mishkan depicted in relation to the threefold division of the world, such that the courtyard corresponds to the sea, the Holy Place to the land, and the Holy of Holies to the heavens. The veil separating the Holy of Holies from the Holy Place consisted of four kinds of thread which were said to correspond to the four elements. And the menorah was viewed as representing the 'lights in the firmament of heaven'.

One of the more elaborate discussions of correspondences in later literature is that written by Malbim in his treatise, 'The Secrets of the Mishkan'. This work focuses on the correspondences between the Mishkan and the human body. For Malbim, the archetypal human form, designated by the Hebrew, 'adam, is the central glyph of creation. The whole of creation thus takes the form of a great, or cosmic, Adam, all parts of which resonate with their counterparts in the individual person. He gives an image of the strings on a small harp resonating in response to the sounding of the strings of a large one. The Mishkan is viewed as depicting this archetypal pattern in intricate detail.

THE HOLY OF HOLIES

Malbim first considers the Holy Ark. Inside the Ark were four compartments, two above two. The lower two housed the broken pieces of the original tablets of stone given by God to Moses. These were broken when Moses found the Children of Israel worshipping the golden calf (see Exodus 32). The second, unbroken set of tablets was kept in the upper two compartments. Malbim considers these sets of stones to parallel the brain, with the twin cerebral hemispheres corresponding to the unbroken set above, and the two cerebella beneath corresponding to the broken set below.

To appreciate the meaning and implications of the parallels Malbim draws, one must see them within the context of the

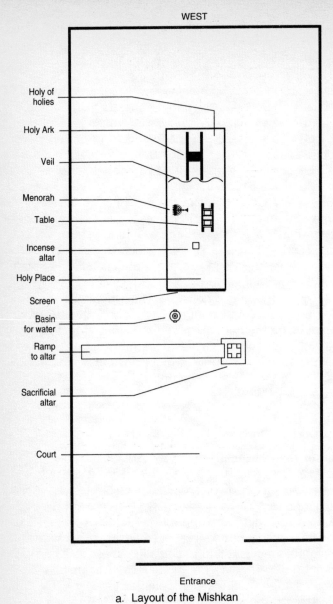

a. Layout of the Mishkan

Figure 2. Layout of the Mishkan and its furnishings

entire Mishkan as a complete 'living' system. As far as the Ark is concerned, we are dealing with the highest that is attainable in our world – the point of contact with the divine. The tablets of stone inside embody the revelation from God, and attached to the top of the Ark was the 'seat' of communion with God. The parallel which Malbim draws between the Ark and the brain concerns the nature of wisdom. The stones comprise the Torah which is the source of wisdom in the world, whilst the brain is the source of wisdom in the body. The Ark encapsulates the intelligence upon which the logic of the whole structure and operation of the Mishkan is based. If it were absent, the Mishkan as a spiritual meeting place would cease to exist, just as the individual would die without the brain, and – in rabbinic thought – the world would not endure without the Torah.

Malbim elaborates on the correspondence between the structure of the Ark, which housed the stones, and the coverings of the brain. There were three layers to the Ark – an inner gold layer, a middle one of wood, and an outer gold layer. These, he argues, parallel the three brain meninges – the hard dura mater, soft arachnoid membrane, and hard pia mater.

An interesting feature of the Ark concerns the poles used for carrying it. The whole Mishkan was a transportable structure and several of its furnishings were provided with rings for carrying poles. What is distinctive about the Ark is that the poles were not simply useful appendages but central to its symbolism. Unlike those for the altars and the table, they were never removed ('the poles shall be in the rings of the Ark; they shall not be removed from it', Exodus 25:15). Indeed, one tradition holds that the poles used for carrying the Ark were actually a separate set from those attached while it was stationary, thus emphasizing the distinctively symbolic meaning of the latter set.

Malbim sees these two poles as depicting the two senses necessary for receiving Torah. First, vision is needed in order that the written text can be examined. Second, hearing is needed so that the oral tradition may be received. The poles are the nerves emanating from the brain to these two senses.

They are essential and never to be removed, for the Torah can never be static. It cannot rest untouched in a chest, but must penetrate into the real world through those who receive it via eyes and ears. In this context it is interesting to note that in the Mishkan these poles extended into the veil, causing it to bulge out into the Holy Place. The innermost sanctuary – the Holy of Holies – is not to be isolated, cut off from the world in some cave of spiritual narcissism. In Jewish thinking, any spirituality of value must of necessity reach into, and enliven, the world.

THE HOLY PLACE

The Holy of Holies, in which the Ark resided, parallels the head in Adam. The Holy Place parallels the chest region. The two items of furniture in the Holy Place find their counterparts in the two major organs of the chest: the heart and lungs. The table served to display the special loaves, or shewbread. In this way its function depicted nourishment, which Malbim sees as a point of connection to the heart since the heart was viewed as nourishing the body through the blood. The placing of bread on the table in the Mishkan was supposed to draw a blessing from God and thus to ensure general sustenance. A somewhat deeper idea is conveyed by the double meaning of the Hebrew, *panim*, in the word for shewbread. The English 'shew' presumably derives from the first meaning which is 'face'. The second meaning is 'inward', suggesting to Malbim that the real sustenance is inward, or spiritual, and derives from study of the words of Torah. In his scheme, whilst the brain is the source of wisdom, paralleling Torah itself, it is the heart which enables the individual to assimilate the meaning of the words of Torah. The heart is viewed as the seat of understanding. Thus, for example, in the book of Proverbs, Wisdom says to those who are 'lacking in heart' (that is, lacking understanding), 'come, eat of my bread' (Proverbs 9:4–5) – partake of the wisdom in the Torah. Understanding involves making something one's own, knowing it throughout one's whole body, and is aptly symbolized by the heart which is the centre of the whole body.

Bread

Bread is the symbolic food *par excellence*. It epitomizes the intended relationship between God and humankind. Whilst the wheat grows as a 'gift from God', it is only through our own hard effort that bread can be produced. The parallel with Torah should be clear. The Torah is a gift from God. But its words are largely empty unless we work hard to effect our own connection to them. Refining the wheat, kneading the dough, passing through fire – each is a stage with a precise parallel in the spiritual journey involved in acquiring Torah. As quoted already in Chapter 2, 'According to the effort is the reward'. When we read the saying of R. Elazar ben Azariah that, 'If there is no flour, there is no Torah; if there is no Torah, there is no flour',[8] the meaning is not simply that one has to eat in order to have the strength to study. R. Elazar ben Azariah is cryptically alluding to this more inward parallel between Torah and bread which underlies the spiritual significance of the table in the Holy Place of the Mishkan.

The Menorah

The other organ in the chest region is the lung, which Malbim relates to the menorah in the Holy Place. The menorah, as a seven-branched lampstand, alludes to the seven days of creation through which the Torah becomes manifest in the world. Torah is transcendent wisdom which is concealed in the diversity of forms created through the seven days: 'Wisdom has built her house; she has hewn out her seven pillars', as the book of Proverbs puts it. From the human point of view, it is our intellect which ideally reveals the patterns of the transcendent wisdom in those worldly forms, as it does also in the words of scripture. The menorah, then, stands for the intellect – the light of reason. The parallel with the lungs may seem a little odd to us today. But for Malbim, the lungs played a crucial spiritual role in our intellectual life. They were viewed as complementing the heart by purifying the air of breath and directing the resulting spiritual vapour upwards towards the brain.

These two items of furniture, the table and menorah, represent respectively the bodily (heart) and the intellectual (lungs) dimensions of the human soul. Just as the lungs and heart are situated together in one cavity, so are the table and menorah together in one compartment of the Mishkan. Just as the heart is displaced to the left, and the lungs to the right, in the human body, so we find the positioning of table and menorah to the left (north) and right respectively in the Holy Place.

There is a great deal of profound symbolism in the menorah which I can only touch upon briefly here. This was the only item in the Mishkan made with no material other than pure gold. It was 'drawn out' from one single piece of gold symbolically representing the way in which the seed of intelligence grows within a person. The relation to the lungs mentioned above concerns the mystical identification of breath with the intellectual soul in humans ('And the Lord God formed Adam, dust from the ground, and He breathed into his nostrils the spirit of life and Adam became a living soul', Genesis 2:7). The pattern of the menorah is clearly that of a plant reaching upwards; the side-arms are referred to as branches and its ornamentations are based on the form of flowers. The symbolism should be clear: the menorah is the individual human soul, untarnished by base material, striving upwards to blossom forth in its encounter with the emanations of God which are depicted by the seven lights themselves.

Figure 3 portrays the basic form of the menorah as the oral tradition has recorded it. An interesting aspect of its symbolism may be explored with reference to the positioning of its ornamentations. Its height is 18 *tefachim*, 'handbreadths'. This is the gematria of the Hebrew *hai*, meaning 'life'. The ornamentations represent the stages of our spiritual ascent through a lifetime. The first flower comes after one sixth of its full height. This depicts the completion, or 'flowering', of childhood. This ornamentation is of flower petals only. If a lifetime were taken as 72 years, then this flowering is at 12 years. The first 'complete' ornamentation comes at a point one third of the way to its full height. The three symbolic ornamentations are included. These are the flower-cup (calyx), flower-bowl (reproductive capsule) and flower petals (corolla). Symbolically, then, whilst the flowering of childhood is aiming ever higher up the career ladder, or one's energies become directed more towards spiritual goals. In kabbalistic thought, the latter choice – the spiritual journey – means encountering the seven lower sefirot, which are represented as the seven branches of the menorah.

The branches of the menorah begin at this half-way point, and represent the individual's initiation into the spiritual reality of the sefirot. Beneath each branch is a flower-bowl representing this storing up of one's potential. In order to receive an influx from a particular sefirah, appropriate meditations and studies must be pursued. The energy directed into such endeavours is akin to the plant's energy which is focused for reproductive purposes in the flower-bowl. Unlike the flowering of adulthood described above, however, this energy gives no immediate flower. It is the energy we require to 'branch out' towards a particular sefirah. The flower only comes in the final encounter with the essence of that sefirah.

The twenty-two flower-cups symbolize the twenty-two letters of the Hebrew alphabet. Each letter depicts a separate quality in the spiritual world. In later kabbalistic symbolism these become the twenty-two paths of the tree of life (see Chapter 5). In the symbolism of the menorah only one of these aspects is experienced in mundane adulthood; the other twenty-one await the spiritual traveller in encounters with the essence of each of the seven sefirot.

THE OUTER COURT

Returning now to the scheme as depicted by Malbim, the third division of the Mishkan, the outer court, is viewed as paralleling the abdominal cavity in Adam. In the outer court stood the bronze altar. A parallel may be drawn between the functions of this altar and those of the human digestive system. In general terms the sacrificial process was understood to release the inner 'soul' of the animal from its physical clothing. It is not difficult to perceive the connection between this and the concept of the digestive system releasing the inner sustenance from the physicality of food. Many quite specific parallels are drawn not only to the digestive system as a whole, but also to its various parts. Just as the altar required many utensils to support its functions, so too with the stomach. Thus, bowls to hold the blood of sacrifices correspond to the liver in the body; pots for getting rid of ashes correspond to the colon conveying waste matter; and so the list continues into quite intricate detail.

This is merely a selection of the correspondences expounded in the 'Secrets of the Mishkan'. What becomes clear through the great emphasis on detail is the overwhelming sense of the Mishkan as a 'living' system. It is not simply a structure which depicts a higher order; it brings that higher order into harmonious rapport with our more mundane physical reality. The Mishkan in operation becomes the meeting place of heaven and earth. And, with the establishment of a fixed site in Jerusalem, the Temple service became the focus of all Jewish endeavour for the best part of a thousand years.

THE HOLINESS OF SHABBAT

For the practically two thousand years since the destruction of Jerusalem, however, Judaism has survived without its Temple. It has been largely due to the holiness of Shabbat as a vehicle for the same aspirations as were embodied in the Temple practices that Judaism's spiritual heart has continued to beat. The rich symbolism of the Temple finds its counterpart in the rites of Shabbat.

The Hebrew for 'holy', *kadosh*, comes from a root meaning 'to set apart'. And this is the essence of Shabbat – a day is set apart from regular passing time; Shabbat is our connection with eternity. It parallels the holy space of the Temple. Its beginning and end are marked with ceremonies involving fire and wine, just as the limits of a 'magical' space may be marked symbolically with fire and/or water. At the beginning of Shabbat candles are lit and 'kiddush' is recited over wine. With the departure of Shabbat the 'havdalah' ceremony similarly includes special blessings over fire and wine.

The meaning of Shabbat is, of course, founded in the original biblical concept of the seventh day. It is not simply the absence of work which is the crucial feature of the day, but the presence of holiness: 'And God blessed the seventh day and made it holy' (Genesis 2:3). The other six days are bound up with specifics; the seventh is concerned with the whole, and with the possibility of embuing creation with holiness.

The Hebrew root *kadosh*, 'holy', finds expression in the word 'betrothal', *kadesh*. Rabbinic sources on Shabbat are rich in their use of the imagery of love and sexual union with the bride. Shabbat *is* the bride; and the Jewish people become the partner to the seventh day in what amounts to a spiritual marriage. An intimation of this relationship is found by the rabbis in the Torah. One of the major biblical references to Shabbat, in Exodus 31:13–17, is followed by the somewhat peculiar phrase, 'And He gave unto Moses when He finished (*ke-chaloto*) speaking . . . .' The Midrash explains that this word, *ke-chaloto*, means also 'as his bride'. Such is the special relationship with the female presence of God, the Shekhinah, which is enjoyed through observance of Shabbat.

Shabbat is the very essence of holiness within Jewish thinking. It is 'a sign between Me and you throughout your generations that I, The Lord, make you holy' (Exodus 31:13). The concept of a sign needs some elucidation here. For Judaism, a sign is not simply something which happens to represent another in a random fashion. The biblical sign is an embodiment of a higher truth in our, lower, world. The word for sign in Hebrew, *'ot*, has the first letter of the alphabet, *'alef*, linked to the last, *tav*. That which is purely spiritual, transcending physicality (*'alef*), becomes linked (the second letter, *vav*, implies conjunction) to materiality (*tav*). In the case of Shabbat, it does not merely symbolize that there is more to life than the ebb and flow of physical reality; Shabbat itself *is* the other reality. It is a reality defined by holiness and eternity. Shabbat itself, if we can but realize it, *is* a portion of the 'world to come', which is the phrase the rabbis use to refer to the purely spiritual realm.

For the observant Jew, the mind is taken away from practical matters on Shabbat – there are no reports to write, no office to attend, no cooking to be done, no jobs around the house to catch up with. From the outside, it is a day of limitations, of 'thou shalt nots'. But on the inside there is a flurry of activity, for it is a day on which the mind moves towards its transcendent source – through prayer, study and meditation. It is such transcendence which brings about the union with the Shekhinah, mentioned above.

THE LAWS OF CARRYING

With this in mind we may constructively consider an important lesson conveyed by the tractate of the Talmud dealing with Shabbat. It opens with a discussion of the laws of 'carrying'. In brief, the law holds that on Shabbat one may not carry any object, no matter how light, from a private domain (for example, a house) to a public domain (for example, a street) or vice versa.

Following this discussion, the Talmud takes a logical progression through the issues of Shabbat, commencing with matters to do with Friday afternoon, proceeding to consider the kindling of the special Shabbat lights, and so on. The question is, why does the tractate begin as it does, with the subject of 'carrying'? This topic seems to be out of sequence and in any case would be regarded by many as somewhat peripheral, or even trivial.

The answer is that this idea of 'carrying' actually goes to the heart of the Jewish concept of Shabbat. Shabbat primarily depicts not simply the absence of work but a condition in which there are no changes of state – that is, no creativity – involving the physical world. Often these two ideas seem to be synonymous. Thus, if I have to rub two sticks together to make fire, I am certainly engaged in considerable effort and, if successful, the sticks undergo a change of state. If, however, we consider turning a switch to put on electric lights, there is clearly no labour involved. Orthodox Judaism nevertheless rules this latter act as profaning Shabbat, because it brings about a change of state – the element in the bulb changes from a 'non-fiery' state to a 'fiery' one.

The clearest example of this matter is that of 'carrying', for here there is no question of labour. Lifting and carrying an object is not in itself classed as prohibited on Shabbat. So the only issue is whether the object undergoes a change of state or not. The rabbis ruled that if an object were carried, for example, from the house to the street, then a significant change had occurred. Now, to most modern people, having a predominantly materialistic outlook, it may seem that an object is the same object wherever it is. However, the worldview of the rabbis is more mind-centred, especially with regard to Shabbat. It is not the object itself that is important here but how I relate to it. And in this sense, an object is changed in its relationship to me when I move between domains. A key, for example, may take on a different meaning to me depending where I am. When I am outside my house it carries a more active meaning than it does when I am inside. Furthermore, there may be a change in presumed ownership of an object, depending whether it were found in a private or public domain.

THE CREATIVE PROCESS

In a deeper sense the laws of carrying come first because they hint at what actually comes first in the creative process itself. The private domain represents an extension of oneself, the domain within which one's individuality is expressed. Mapped onto the cosmic scale of creativity, it depicts that oneness which underlies the manifest world. In the public domain, on the other hand, individuality is lost; there is only multiplicity. The public domain then corresponds to the multiplicity which is generated from the original oneness in the act of creation. The Hebrew alphabet can be our guide to understanding this idea more clearly. Manifest creation begins in the Torah with the letter *bet*, the first letter of *bere'shit*, 'in the beginning'. This is an explosive letter (as is the English 'b') which is understood as depicting the outpouring of creative potential into the manifest world of multiplicity. But this outpouring is not itself the absolute beginning. Before *bet* in the alphabet comes *'alef*, the silent first letter. Behind all creative endeavour lies the silence of 'inspiration', the oneness behind multiplicity.

In this scheme, *'alef* represents the private domain, *bet*, the public domain. Combining these first two letters gives *'av*, the word for 'father' – symbol of the first stage of creativity.[9] It is the masculine principle which initiates a creative process. In order for this initial spark to develop, however, it must be introduced into a different 'private domain' – the feminine. Clearly, in this symbolism sexuality becomes the paradigm of all creativity. A moment's reflection should convince the reader that it is no mere coincidence then that the Hebrew for 'to enter' (*ba*') comprises the same two letters in the sequence *bet* followed by *'alef*.

FORTY MINUS ONE

A final idea which can cast substantial light on the inner meaning of Shabbat may be gleaned from the talmudic phraseology of the prohibitions on Shabbat. As we saw earlier, page 34, there are 'forty minus one' general categories of creative work which are prohibited. Why number them in this cumbersome fashion; why not thirty-nine?

Number symbolism is central to much of Jewish philosophy and practice. The number forty conveys a particular symbolic significance. That this significance is especially relevant to Shabbat is hinted at more than once in the Torah. One device employed by the Torah to convey its meaning involves numerical codes. The Torah is not divided into sentences; the only meaningful divisions are those into various kinds of block. Sometimes we find that these blocks are composed of such a number of words as to cryptically illuminate the subject matter. Thus, on more than one occasion a block concerned with Shabbat consists of exactly forty words (Exodus 35:1–3; Leviticus 23:1–3).

Forty stands for purification and subsequent renewal in a higher state. In Hebrew the number forty is conveyed by the letter *mem* which itself means water. The symbolism of water in purification rituals and renewal – 'rebirth' – is universal. In the Torah we find Moses dwelling forty days and nights on Mount Sinai, a period during which he becomes imbued with the new revelation. The Children of Israel spend forty years wandering in the wilderness, a period required for a 'new' generation to arise which is not conditioned by the mentality of slavery.

As we have seen, the thirty-nine restrictions on Shabbat correspond to the 'building' of a temple. This correspondence gives a framework of meaning which lends this day its peculiar potency. But the correspondence is only complete when the fortieth level is included. For the Mishkan, this level was achieved by consecration to its higher purpose: 'And you shall take the anointing oil and anoint the Mishkan and all that is in it; and you shall hallow it and all its vessels; and it shall be holy' (Exodus 40:9). The fortieth element for Shabbat corresponds to the role played by this anointing oil in relation to the Mishkan. What is it that finally makes the seventh day holy? The outward sign is the *kiddush*, recited over wine. But ultimately it is the inward aspect that is needed – our own consciousness of the divine. The thirty-nine prohibitions can be legislated for, laid out in full for all to be clear of the details. The fortieth can only be hinted at; it is up to each individual to reach for that transcendent spark that makes their Shabbat holy, and to receive accordingly the spirit of renewal.

4 · HALAKHAH: THE WAY OF HOLINESS

In Jewish tradition great emphasis is placed on the response of the Children of Israel to the first public reading of the Torah: 'And [Moses] took the book of the covenant and read in the ears of the people, and they said: 'All that the Lord has spoken we will do and we will understand' (Exodus 24:7). First there is a commitment to act in accord with the will of God; and second, a willingness to study the word of God. Judaism extracts from the devine revelation its rules of conduct which reach into all spheres of life. But blind faith is insufficient. Study is required in order to understand exactly how the rules apply in specific situations. Through such study one may also glimpse something of the purpose underlying the system of rules. One begins to discern the ways in which the rules ensure the fullest possible awareness of the divine in all walks of life. Indeed, to count as a religion, a way of life requires more than just an agreed set of ethical or philosophical teachings. It must introduce a sense of some kind of transcendent reality into that life. For Judaism this is achieved in practical terms through 'Halakhah', its system of rules.

The term, 'Halakhah', derives from a verbal root meaning 'to walk' or 'go'. It conveys the complex of ideas which Judaism holds about the nature of life itself. If lived in accord with the principles laid out in the Torah, all of life becomes a means of 'walking' in ways that articulate the spiritual reality of the world. Halakhah comprises the 613 *mitzvot*, 'divine commandments', derived from the Torah. Many of these relate to practices no longer current, such as those connected with sacrifices in Temple times. In effect, modern Orthodox Judaism comprises some two hundred mitzvot which relate to practically every circumstance in daily life. There is no distinction between religious and secular life in Judaism. Judaism lays down a complete way of life into which the Halakhah introduces a spiritualizing element. Ideally, the spiritualizing element is present whatever one is engaged in, be it praying, eating, doing business and so on. Halakhah is not simply a set of rules, however. The term refers to the organic body of discussion and teaching which enables the bald recipes in the Torah itself to be made relevant to the particularities of life. Halakhah is very much the bridge between Torah and the real world in which we live.

ACHIEVING HOLINESS

Chapter 19 of Leviticus conveys a central message of the Torah: 'You shall be holy for I the Lord your God am holy' (19:2). Halakhah – the means of achieving holiness in life – is bound up with the intention of imitating God. The rabbis often stated, for example, that one should act compassionately because God Himself is compassionate. Thus, the Talmud explains the phrase, '. . . you shall keep the mitzvot of the Lord your God and walk in His ways' (Deuteronomy 28:9), as enjoining us to walk after His compassionate attributes: 'Just as He clothes the naked . . . so should you clothe the naked; just as He visits the sick . . . so should you visit the sick; just as He comforts mourners . . . so should you comfort mourners; just as He buries the dead . . . so should you bury the dead'.[1] The centrality of this concept of the imitation of God was stressed by the second-century-C.E. sage, Ben Azzai, who considered the statement of Genesis 5:1 ('This is the book of the generations of Adam, in the day that God created Adam. In the image of God made He him') to be the great principle of Torah.[2] The whole basis of the Halakhah would be impossible were it not for this relationship whereby humankind reflects God Himself.

Included in Leviticus 19 is the famous injunction to 'Love your neighbour as yourself' (19:18). The comment of Ben Azzai is mentioned in the context of R. Akiva's complementary view that it is this injunction which constitutes the great principle of the Torah. The two views convey the two sides of the one coin which is Halakhah. R. Akiva's position is that conduct with one's fellows is paramount; ethical conduct in the social sphere brings holiness in its wake. Ben Azzai, on the other hand, places imitation of God first. One is holy as a consequence of imitating God. Ethical conduct is a consequence of such imitation because God's conduct represents the ideal.

THE FOUR CUBITS

A talmudic sage, R. Hiyya bar Ammi said in the name of Ulla: 'Since the day when the Temple was destroyed, the Holy One, blessed be He, has nothing in His world other than the four cubits of Halakhah'.[3] This somewhat cryptic statement conveys the role Halakhah plays in the scheme of things. As we saw in the last chapter, the Temple carries the blueprint of the higher, spiritual, world. As is the case with the human form also, its very structure conveys holiness to the world.

R. Ammi is informing us that Halakhah plays the same role as did the Temple in bringing holiness to the world. We can explain the significance of the four cubits in the following way; the number four depicts extension (the four points of the compass) as well as the four elements of matter. It therefore indicates something with a tangible place in our physical world. It is central to Jewish thinking that the abstract is insufficient as a basis for spirituality. Halakhah can sometimes involve subtle analysis of the minutiae of the Torah and may begin to appear somewhat abstract. But it is always directed to a real, physical aim – how to act in the world in accord with the divine scheme. It is therefore symbolized in terms of four cubits. Halakhah is comparable to the Temple in its role of enabling the presence of the higher world to be expressed through the physicality of the lower.

In this talmudic statement the number four is conveyed by the Hebrew letter *dalet*. The word *dalet* means 'door'. Indeed, the very shape of the letter depicts the opening of a door. These concrete images carry Judaism's essential vision, namely that our world of physical extension is merely a door to the concealed, higher world. Halakhah is the key which opens that door.

THE INTENTION OF THE LAW

In the previous chapter I discussed the significance of Shabbat. The relationships between the macrocosm, the human form, the Temple and Shabbat convey many deep insights of a mystical and philosophical nature. Whilst rabbinic Judaism hints at these insights, it clearly focuses on the practical questions. The Halakhah determines what an individual may and may not do in a specific situation. Thus, in relation to Shabbat, for example, there are details concerning the precise time when candles should be lit to 'welcome' Shabbat; what materials the candles may be made from; how long they should burn; who should light them; etc. And all other aspects of Shabbat observance come under similar scrutiny. Every little detail becomes a matter which has been the subject of rabbinic discussion and ruling. Indeed, Judaism has often been criticized for burying its spiritual insights under cumbersome levels of detailed regulations. It may appear that the 'letter of the law' dislodges the 'spirit of the law'.

The intention of Halakhah, however, is not to confine people by innumerable detailed laws the to align their lives with the higher plan revealed by God in the Torah. The mitzvot represent the outer face of Torah as it is manifest in the physical world of everyday life. The rabbinic understanding may be illustrated by a Midrash based on an ambiguity in a famous phrase in the book of Micah. Micah summarizes the

Torah: 'He has told you, Adam, what is good and what the Lord seeks from you. It is to do justice, to love kindness, and to walk humbly with your God' (Micah 6:8). The ambiguity comes in the final command, 'to walk humbly' with God. The word translated as 'humbly' (*hatznai'a*) correctly means 'to conceal'. It is understood that the text implies that Halakhah ('walking') becomes a covering – a concealment – to spiritual meaning. It is a covering designed not to block out the deeper meaning but, on the contrary, to enable individuals to arrive at these deeper meanings in their own time and in their own ways. Without the halakhic perspective, there is the danger that 'pearls cast before swine' simply excite ephemeral interest.

CONCEALMENT AND REVELATION

Whatever else may be said about it, Judaism is certainly the master of concealment. In part, this came about through the exigencies of oppression. Through the major part of its post-biblical history Judaism has been a religion surrounded by hostile elements. Concealing its deeper teachings became a means of protection. It would, however, be wrong to suggest that concealment is a product of oppression alone. It is intrinsic both to Judaism's understanding of the Torah and also to its approach to human psychology. These two factors elucidate the emphasis Judaism places on the Halakhah, for Halakhah brings the whole person into the process of revelation itself.

At Judaism's core lies a paradox concerning the nature of revelation. Revelation is not an unchecked revealing. If all were revealed, there would be no further role for humankind. As we saw in Chapter 1, the whole point of God's revelation was that human endeavour should be directed at elucidating the meaning of Torah. God conceals the spiritual world within the Torah's stories and commandments at the same time as proffering the means, through those words themselves, for us to uncover their hidden spiritual content:

R. Levi, in the name of R. Hama bar Hanina commenced thus: 'It is the glory of God to conceal a thing, but the glory of

kings is to search out a matter' (Provers 25:2) ... It is
the glory of words of Torah, which are likened to kings,
as it is said, 'By me kings reign' (Proverbs 8:15), to search
out a matter.[4]

By means of the revelation God has set in motion a process
which it is up to us to complete. The very *playing* with the
Hebrew text, so characteristic of rabbinic thought, is itself a
human continuation of the revelation. As such, it is intrinsically valuable. Indeed, such playing furthers the imitation of
God who is Himself described as 'playing' with Torah before
creation. But there is a further intention behind revelation,
namely that the Torah should reach to earth. Searching out
the meanings of the text in terms of its tangible implications for
action, and bringing it into the physical world by performance
of the mitzvot so determined, completes the revelation. The
paradox of revelation endures, however, since the mitzvot are
themselves a concealment of the Torah's inner teaching.

THE THRONE OF GLORY

Judaism expresses this point through numerous stories indicating that the Torah's role is here on earth, not in heaven. In
one, for example, the angels are astonished at God's intention
to give the 'secret treasure' of Torah to creatures of flesh and
blood. God requires of Moses that he should answer the
angels. Moses holds on to the Throne of Glory (ostensibly
for protection) and answers to the effect that the contents
of Torah relate specifically to human, not angelic, life. The
Torah's commands concerning Shabbat, for example, or the
laws prohibiting murder and stealing, all relate to human life
in this world and are of no consequence to the angels in their
purely spiritual abode.[5]

The Throne of Glory stands for the essence of the higher
world. The message of this story is conveyed by the image of
Moses holding on to the Throne of Glory whilst answering the
angels in terms of the Torah's relation to our physical world.
The revelation is indeed a secret treasure, comprising the

deepest knowledge of the higher world. But God's purpose is not fulfilled until it is manifest through actions in the physical world. God's intention was that Torah should enable the physical world to be sanctified. As expressed by a rabbinic authority of our day, Joseph Soloveitchik:

> Holiness, according to the outlook of Halakhah, denotes the appearance of a mysterious transcendence in the midst of our concrete world, the 'descent' of God, whom no thought can grasp, onto Mount Sinai, the bending down of a hidden and concealed world and lowering it onto the face of reality.[6]

AKHNAI'S OVEN

That the place of Torah is here on earth and not in heaven is illustrated by the talmudic story of Akhnai's oven. In brief, there was a disagreement between R. Eliezer and the rest of the rabbis over the halakhic state of the oven – was it or was it not ritually 'clean'? R. Eliezer called on 'heavenly powers' to support his view. Despite the fact that these powers agreed with R. Eliezer, the halakhic ruling followed the majority. It is for earthly rabbis to decide the Halakhah democratically; heavenly forces would constitute an intrusion:

> [R. Eliezer] said to them: 'If the Halakhah agrees with me, let this carob tree prove it'. The carob tree was uprooted and hurled from its place . . . 'No proof can be brought from a carob tree', they said to him. Again he said to them: 'If the Halakhah agrees with me, let the stream of water prove it'. The stream of water flowed backwards. 'No proof can be brought from a stream of water', they said . . . R. Eliezer persisted: 'If the Halakhah agrees with me, let it be proved from heaven'. A heavenly voice went forth and said: 'Why do you dispute with R. Eliezer, since in every detail the Halakhah agrees with him!' R. Joshua stood up and exclaimed: 'It [Torah] is not in heaven' (Deuteronomy 30:12). What did he mean? R. Jeremiah said: 'It has already been given on Mount Sinai. We pay no attention to a heavenly voice since You [God] already wrote in the Torah at Mount Sinai. "Follow the majority in judgements" [a rabbinic interpretation of Exodus 23:2].' R.

Nathan met Elijah and asked him: 'How did the Holy One, blessed be He, then react?' He replied: 'He laughed and said, "My sons have defeated me, my sons have defeated me!"'[7]

RIGHT CONDUCT

When it comes to human psychology, Halakhah emphasizes the holism which unifies physical action and spiritual purpose. It is for this reason that any tendency towards asceticism has generally been resisted. Judaism is a 'this-worldly' religion. As the short prayer associated with performance of a mitzvah puts it, God 'has sanctified us through His mitzvot'. Holiness, for Judaism, comes through proper conduct – conduct that is in accord with Torah – in this world. Indeed, foregoing the pleasures available in this world can be contrary to the spirit of Judaism.

In terms that seem consistent with a modern approach, Judaism sees the person as a complex of physical, psychological, and spiritual levels of action. Of the three, the rabbis saw the psychological as the weak link, since arrogance and delusion can deflect a person from right conduct. This attitude is apparent, for example, in discussions as to whether an appropriate intention is necessary when performing a mitzvah. Although appropriate intentions are valuable, the general rabbinic view is that the physical deed itself can be sufficient, even if performed in an automatic, mechanical way. Observance is the most important thing. In one sense this reflects a somewhat dependent attitude: God has His reasons for the mitzvot, and it is for us simply to do as instructed. More profoundly, however, it expresses the value the rabbis placed on physical action as the vehicle for actualizing spiritual purpose.

This is precisely the issue on which Judaism parted company with Hellenism. The Hellenistic outlook saw the psychological and spiritual realms as largely contiguous, but as being essentially separate from the physical. To a large degree, this outlook came to dominate the way in which most westerners see the nature of reality down to our day. In particular, it influenced the early Christians in their view that many biblical commands were merely allegorical, pertaining not to physical action but to spiritual matters only. Nowhere is this divergence from Jewish thought more pronounced than in relation to the command of circumcision. For Christianity, the biblical requirement is for a 'circumcised heart', a state of mental humility and spiritual openness with no need for physical circumcision. For Judaism, the deepest spiritual value of this 'sign of the covenant' is totally bound up with its physical embodiment. The physical and spiritual realms are holistically interrelated. The Hellenistic worldview, which drove a wedge between these two realms, was thus antithetical to Judaism. Perhaps the greatest of Hebrew poets, Judah Ha-Levi (eleventh to twelfth century), writes: 'Let not Greek wisdom tempt you, for it bears flowers only and no fruit'. For Judaism, the danger of Hellenism was apparent in the two extremes of either glorifying the body for its own sake (Olympic ideal) or denigrating the body for the sake of some spiritual purpose (asceticism). Furthermore, the Hellenistic outlook leads to a rarification of the spiritual as pertaining only to the soul (or mind) and not to the body. It divorces God from the world of the here-and-now.

THE TALMUD

Perhaps the deepest insight into the nature of Judaism will be found through examining a page or two of the Talmud. The very structure of this work depicts something of the psychology of Judaism. As the record of rabbinic discussions over several hundred years up until the fifth century C. E., the Talmud has a very real dynamic. It is a work that lends itself to oral study, the discussions seeming to come alive as one enters into its arguments and stories. Whilst a major aim of the Talmud is to establish the Halakhah, the arguments, diverse opinions, stories and homilies generate a complex sea of words which at times almost seem to distract from the halakhic imperative. The Talmud is like an externalized stream of consciousness. Its sea of words generated by diverse minds, parallels the sea of words and images generated, perhaps at an unconscious level, in the individual human mind.

The logical deductions in the Talmud, which are directed towards formulating the Halakhah, parallel the conscious flow of thought in the individual, characterized as it is by 'reality orientation'. As psychology has demonstrated, however, this conscious stream is constantly influenced, jostled, as it were, by unconscious activity 'deeper' in the mind. So too in the Talmud. In the middle of a logical flow, for example, a diverse association will be explored; names will trigger further aphorisms; a play on words reveals new meanings; words or phrases are treated as fragments with no reference to time or context. And at any point a whole bizarre myth, perhaps of giant sea creatures or magical events, may erupt. As the work of Freud, Jung and others has shown, all these styles of mentation are characteristic of the impact unconscious material may have on the flow of consciousness.

The way in which a coherent whole is somehow forged in the Talmud from the diverse contributions of rabbis – sometimes hundreds of years apart and from distant locations – mysteriously parallels the way in which the self in the individual emerges despite the multiplicity and diversity of mental processes. In the Talmud, within the almost seething mass of words there are two fixed points with which no-one can argue. The inner fixed point is provided by scripture. Whatever the issue under consideration, ideas are constantly related back to the words of the Bible, the divine source which is the ultimate root of the entire work. The outer fixed point is the mitzvah – concrete action in the physical world.

The psychological thrust of discussion and anecdote falls into place between these two roots – between the spiritual world of revealed scripture and the physical world of action. As it is in a page of Talmud, so is it in the person: Halakhah seeks to unite the physical and the spiritual, bringing the psychological into its rightful place between them.

The psychological force of Halakhah is thus profound indeed:

R. Yohanan said: Whoever keeps the Torah truly it is accounted by Scripture as though he had made himself, for it is written, 'And the Lord commanded me at this time to teach you statutes and judgements to do them' (Deuteronomy 4:14). The text does not say 'to do them' but 'to make yourselves with them' – this implies that he is accounted as though he had made and created himself.[8]

As R. Soloveitchik writes in relation to Halakhah: 'The most fundamental principle of all is that man must create himself'.[9]

CODIFYING THE LAW

It is a common observation within psychology that mere insight into a problem is not in itself sufficient to bring about some desired change. The insight needs to be brought down to earth in some way. Therapies may focus on 'acting out' or use some kind of modelling technique. When a child who has been the victim of some form of abuse, for example, can begin to depict a way back to wholesome relationships in clay models or painting, their recovery may be considered to have begun. The emphasis on Halakhah in Judaism bears a similar message. Physical actions speak louder than psychological intentions or thoughts.

Halakhah is concerned with all aspects of life. It covers matters of prayer and festival observance, criminal and civil law, agricultural practice, and so on. Where the Torah lays down a principle, the rabbis were concerned to establish exactly how that principle is obeyed in concrete, practical terms. Moreover, the creative endeavour to determine the Halakhah in given situations did not cease with the closing of the talmudic age. In the mediaeval period, for example, rabbinic authorities issued *responsa*, learned treatises in response to questions concerning specific halakhic matters. In our own day, issues such as medical ethics, or even space exploration, continue to exercise minds attempting to determine what is halakhically correct. There is nothing intrinsically anachronistic about Halakhah. The revelation on Sinai is continually kept alive by applying Torah to the exigencies of one's own day.

As far as Halakhah is concerned, developments in Judaism in the post-talmudic period have been largely concerned with codifying the law and seeking the reasons for the various mitzvot in more systematic fashion than is found in either the Torah or the Talmud. As mentioned above, the Talmud is a veritable sea of discussions. An issue may arise in one place, only to submerge again and reappear somewhere else. On account of its distinctive style, it does not lend itself easily to the need for direct answers to specific questions. In addition, over the centuries much additional material came within the complex sweep of the Halakhah through the many *responsa* issued. As the Jewish communities became more and more dispersed, so the need to maintain a unified body of law became increasingly important. Indeed, Halahkah became the central basis for a continuing common identity amongst Jews in the diaspora. There can be little doubt that the survival of Judaism as a relatively unified religion through its two thousand years of dispersion is largely due to the role played by the Halakhah. The conviction that authentic rulings of law owe their authority to the historically unique revelation on Sinai may seem a somewhat quaint idea, but it is probably the single most important factor in the survival, seemingly against all odds, of Judaism.

Probably the two most important codes of law are the twelfth-century *Mishneh Torah* of Maimonides and the *Shulchan 'Arukh* completed in 1563 by Joseph Caro. Maimonides' goal was to produce a single work which would serve as a ready source for a rabbi to look up the precise rules of conduct in given situations. To achieve this goal, Maimonides saw the need for two major forms of systematization of Halakhah. Firstly, unlike the Talmud, his work would be rigorously divided according to subject matter. Thus, anyone would know exactly where to look for a particular subject. Secondly, a single decision as to what the law is would be recorded. One would not have to wade through lengthy discussions to gain the answer to a specific question.

This second innovation proved to be highly controversial. Many regarded the ebb-and-flow of the talmudical approach to be essential for a rabbi to be able to give an appropriate answer to a halakhic question. The idea that you could rely on a simple book of rules was antithetical to the spirit of the Halakhah itself. Furthermore, Maimonides dispensed with the tradition of citing names and sources in his rulings. To his critics, this compromised the sense of an unbroken line of tradition in the Oral Torah, again something central to the spirit of Halakhah.

The controversy is not only of historical interest. It conveys something of the view of Halakhah within Judaism. A code is essentially a book of rules: it states exactly what to do in a given circumstance. Clearly someone who has facility only with the rule book cannot be compared with one who is at home with all the material from which the rules were extracted. For Judaism, the religious obligation does not involve only determining the Halakhah, that is, determining exactly what to do in a given situation. The purpose of study is to explore the ramifications of the words of Torah as fully as possible. The exploration itself is a vital part of the exercise. All opinions, if validly related to biblical sources, have their place. In traditional language, all discussions and arguments recorded in the Talmud were 'for the sake of heaven'. Often, following a particularly intense divergence of opinion between two sages it is stated that 'these and these [opinions and arguments] are the words of the living God'. God is, as it were, brought to life through the vitality of authentic debate. This is indeed what is meant by the term, Oral Torah: it designates not simply the rules of conduct, but the traditions concerning all potentialities which inhere in the words of the Written Torah.

Maimonides' work is still a major resource in Judaism today. Its lucidity and scope are beyond argument. The specific point of controversy has been met over the years by commentators who have annotated it with appropriate references to sources and proofs for the various rulings. Moreover, study of the Talmud was never really eclipsed by this or any of the other codes.

Caro avoided the same controversy by producing two works. The major one, his *Bet Yosef*, compiles all his sources and explains the derivation of his final rulings on halakhic questions. The *Shulchan 'Arukh* is a separate work which compiles only the rulings themselves. As Caro wrote, this work was produced in order that 'every rule shall be clear in practice'. He certainly achieved this goal and the *Shulchan 'Arukh* continues to be the major source-book for Jewish law used today.

RATIONALISM AND THE MITZVOT

When it comes to adducing reasons for the mitzvot, a certain tension has been evident throughout Jewish history. It is undoubtedly central to human thinking to search out reasons and explanations for things. Many of the greatest rabbinic minds have, accordingly, attempted to give rational or mystical explanations of the mitzvot. Weighed against this, however, has been a reticence to detract from the simple view of the 'yoke of heaven', namely that God's commands need no explanation. Moreover, where a mitzvah is seen to be predicated on a psychological reason there is the danger that people may believe that they can maintain the desired psychological state without adhering to the letter of the law. Judaism tends to see human nature as lacking the perserverence for such integrity. As we saw earlier, it views psychological intention as being potentially something of a weak link in a person's constitution. Thus, the search for reasons can begin a slippery slope leading eventually to compromise on the very principles of the law. This view is articulated in the Talmud in the name of R. Yitzhak:

> Why were reasons for the Torah not revealed? Because the reasons for two scriptural commands were revealed and the greatest man in the world stumbled on account of them. It is written, 'He [a king] shall not multiply wives for himself, that his heart be not turned astray.' (Deuteronomy 17:17). Said Solomon: I shall multiply wives and my heart shall no be turned astray. However, it is written, 'It came to pass when Soloman was old, that his wives turned astray his heart after other gods' (1 Kings 11:4).[10]

Notwithstanding this view of R. Yitzhak, the literature dealing with reasons for the mitzvot is extensive. Judaism attempts to strike a balance between adherence to the law simply because it is God's will, and the quest to uncover the reasons for the mitzvot, which were concealed in the Torah.

The Hebrew phrase generally translated as 'reasons for the mitzvot', *ta'amei ha-mitzvot*, literally means 'flavours of the mitzvot'. This choice of words is important. Any 'reasons' adduced are not presented as arguments for performing a given mitzvah, since observing the mitzvah is a matter of accepting God's will. The 'reasons' are rather 'flavours' which enrich the act. Flavour does not cause us to eat. Eating is essential; but flavour enriches the experience.

Maimonides argues that, as products of God's wisdom, all the mitzvot have a rational basis. Some are obviously designed to promote general well-being and harmony in society (not to murder, steal etc.), whereas others had the effect of weaning the people away from pagan practices. Many of the mitzvot may be viewed as discouraging idolatory in particular. In some of his writings he cites the sacrificial laws, for example, as providing a means to channel the sacrificial desires of a somewhat primitive people. Thus, the sacrifices were hedged in with innumerable legalistic details such that spontaneity was squeezed out. Indeed, only a select few – the priests – could perform the sacrifices, and then only in one place – the Temple. Moreover, the aims of sacrifice were transferred from those involving pagan gods to the One God of monotheism. It should be pointed out that in his thinking on the sacrifices, Maimonides was somewhat at odds with the majority opinion which viewed sacrificial rites as inherently articulating a key element of divine service.

The highest function of the mitzvot, for Maimonides, is to promote the realization of human potential – to enable one to draw near to God's nature. The mitzvot function to purify human character and to lead one towards that intellectual perfection from which knowledge of God implicitly follows. The purification of character is encouraged by the many mitzvot which require the person to be compassionate and non-vindictive. Furthermore, the love of God is inculcated by mitzvot such as 'tefillin' and 'mezzuzah' which surround the observant Jew with signs of God's presence.

It is not only to fellow humans that the Halakhah requires a compassionate stance, and Maimonides strikes a particularly modern-sounding note in his analysis of the laws concerning animals. The Torah forbids killing an animal and its mother on the same day. Similarly, one may not take eggs from a nest while the mother bird is present. These mitzvot, argues Maimonides, ensure that the animals should not suffer unduly. Indeed, he sees all the complex laws of animal slaughter as designed to minimize the pain suffered by animals. Many of the mitzvot clearly instil a healthy respect for other creatures and the natural world as a whole.

MYSTICISM AND THE MITZVOT

Maimonides represents the rationalistic pole in Jewish thought. The other pole is occupied by the mystics who viewed such rationalistic reasons as superficial or even misleading. In a nutshell, the difference between the two is largely one of perspective. For the rationalist, the mitzvot advance human potential but have no influence on God who, as absolute perfection, could have no need of such influence. The mitzvot are solely for the benefit of humankind. The Jewish mystic, by comparison, sees observance of mitzvot not only as influencing ourselves through their immediate character-enhancing nature, but also as impacting on the whole world and even affecting the emanations of God Himself. Such large-scale effects are consequent upon the influence of the mitzvot on the dynamics of the sefirotic realm, the world of divine emanations. For, as is often stated in mystical literature, 'the impulse from below draws forth the impulse from above'. That is, performance of a mitzvah in the lower, physical, world brings about some degree of harmonization in the higher world – the realm of the sefirot – which, in turn, positively influences the world in general as well the one who performed the mitzvah in particular. A 'supernal influx' descends from the sefirotic world into the lower world. In Jewish mysticism, then, the mitzvot are understood as influencing the complex resonances operating throughout the various worlds reaching to the highest world of God's emanations.

For Maimonides, the meaning of the mitzvot is to be found in terms of *this* world; for the mystic their meaning may only be found in terms of the higher, sefirotic, world. Maimonides' approach in this regard contributed substantially to the controversy which followed the dissemination of his works, to which I referred earlier.

A major focus for mystical speculation on the mitzvot arises from their enumeration. R. Simlai is quoted in the Talmud: '613 mitzvot were given to Moses, 365 are prohibitions, corresponding to the number of days in the year and 248 are positive commandments, corresponding to the number of limbs [that is, structures] of man's body'.[11] Later sources equate the number of prohibitions to the number of veins in the body. For the mystic, these numbers illustrate the way in which the halakhic scheme unfolds from a higher reality. The form of man – in the image of God – is the plan of the higher world. The mitzvot form the structure, or body, of the living organism which is Torah. Each limb of the physical human body is reflective of an active 'structure' in the higher world, which is drawn closer to our world through the appropriate mitzvah. As expressed in a kabbalistic text of the thirteenth century, *Sefer ha-Yihud*:

> When the lower man blemishes one of his limbs, as that limb is blemished below, it is as if he cuts the corresponding supernal limb. And the meaning of this cutting is that the limb is cut, and becomes more and more contracted, and is gathered to the depths of being, called nothingness, as if that limb is missing above. For when the human form is perfect below, it brings about perfection above; [in the same manner] the impurity of the limb below causes the gathering of the image of that supernal limb into the depths of nothingness, so as to blemish the supernal form, as it is written, 'Because of the evil, the righteous is taken away' (Isaiah 57:1) – taken away, literally.[12]

The subject here is not physical blemishes! The text is concerned with the mitzvot: neglecting a mitzvah blemishes a 'limb'; observing the mitzvah perfects it. The supernal limb is a portion of the sefirotic realm which is the means for the divine influx to reach the lower worlds. If, therefore, the limb becomes contracted, the divine influx is restricted.

For the mystics, the mitzvot depict the hidden nature of

God, and one's intention in performing the mitzvah should be focused accordingly. Contemplation of the esoteric meaning of the mitzvah becomes a central feature of the religious life. It is not simply a matter of having in mind that one is performing some particular mitzvah in recognition of God's will. For the mystic, the intention incorporates a whole, complex understanding of the sefirotic world and the effects the mitzvah has in that world. Whilst one's immediate religious duty may be fulfilled in a minimal sense by action alone, mystics understand that a more profound responsibility lies on their shoulders. Their actions will effect the limbs of God Himself and certainly require an appropriate understanding of those limbs in relation to the esoteric aspect of the mitzvah. And, since the human form is the microcosm, the key to this understanding lies within. Knowledge of self and knowledge of God are the handmaidens of each mitzvah in the mystic's spiritual arsenal.

It is impossible in a work of this nature to convey the complexity and intricacy with which the relationships between the mitzvot and the higher worlds have been discerned in the mystical tradition. To call elements of a particular mitzvah symbolic hardly does justice to the detail of the hints unravelled by Jewish mystics. A brief discussion of one example will have to suffice. I mentioned earlier the importance for Judaism of the physical act of circumcision by comparison with the mere mental state ('circumcised heart'). It is largely on account of the deep mystical reverberations of circumcision that such a view is asserted.

CIRCUMCISION

Circumcision is seen as being instrumental in bringing about a correct conformation between higher and lower worlds. In the mysticism of the *Zohar*, uncovering the corona of the penis affects the relationship between the sefirot. Prior to circumcision, the tenth sefirah of *malkhut* is covered over so that it cannot fully receive the influx from higher sefirot. This tenth sefirah is the Shekhinah, or divine presence. The Shekhinah is the feminine aspect of God. It is that aspect of the divine which is closest to humankind and with which we become united in reaching our fullest spiritual potential. Symbolically, the Shekhinah is like the moon – it has no light of its own but may shine by the light which it reflects. The *Zohar* holds that religious activity is directed to restoring the balance in the sefirotic world, which will enable the Shekhinah to receive the higher influx. Circumcision is thought of as influencing the sefirotic world by 'uncovering' the Shekhinah, enabling her to become complete by receiving the influx from higher sefirot. Thus, the physical act of circumcision is understood as having an effect on the higher world of God's emanations.

Circumcision involves removal of the foreskin. For the mystics, however, it is not only the physical organ which is thereby uncovered; in the spiritual domain circumcision brings about an uncovering of a rich channel of communication between the worlds. It is significant in this context that Moses is described as having 'uncircumcised lips' (for example, Exodus 7:30). He is so deeply in touch with the higher world that he is unable to communicate directly and fully with those in the lower world. The channel between these worlds – represented here by speech – is not fully open. Hence, Moses operates in conjunction with Aaron as a spokesman. Moses and Aaron together constitute a bridge between the worlds. Whilst Moses' face is directed heavenward, Aaron faces the earthly realm.

The episode of Abraham's circumcision described in Genesis 17 is followed by the statement: 'And the Lord appeared to him in the plains of Mamre and he was sitting in the opening of the tent at the heat of the day'. The 'opening of the tent' is mystically interpreted as the opening in the higher world, so that now, after Abraham's circumcision, the supernal wisdom can flow unhindered through the sefirot and into the Shekhinah, thereby completing, or perfecting, the Shekhinah: 'Before Abraham was circumcised he was closed. When he was circumcised all was revealed and the Shekhinah rested upon him in her completeness'.[13] Just as circumcision was the perfection of Abraham ('Walk before me and be perfect', Genesis 17:1), so is it also the perfecting of the Shekhinah.

In the mystical letter symbolism of the *Zohar*, circumcision uncovers the letter *yod*, the letter depicting the potency of the divine. This symbolism is directed at both the physical appearance of the uncovered corona and also the potency in the upper sefirot: 'Come and see: Abraham was not called perfect with respect to [the sefirah of] *hesed* until the *yod* of the penis was revealed. And when it was revealed, he was called perfect, as it is written, "Walk before me and be perfect".'[14]

In the *Sefer Yetzirah* the covenant of circumcision is mentioned in juxtaposition to the 'covenant of the tongue'. There is indeed a complex spiritual and psychological relationship between these two. In Hebrew, the one word, *milah*, means both 'circumcision' and 'word'. Judaism sees an instructive parallel between the creativity engendered through sexual activity and that pertaining to the ability to use language. Both are harnessed to a higher spiritual potential through the 'covenant' with God, who Himself creates through the power of words. Just as circumcision uncovers the divine potential in the sefirotic realm as discussed above, so the covenant of the tongue grants one access to the potency which inheres in the Hebrew language. In Jewish thought, the two covenants are united in the ultimate human activity – study of Torah. One is only able to understand the deeper meanings of the Torah through a penetration of, or union with, the text. This idea is symbolically conveyed in sexual terms. As Wolfson succinctly puts it, 'The opening of the flesh [circumcision] eventuates in the opening of God, which is reexperienced as the opening of the text'.[15]

In these few paragraphs I have tried to convey something of the flavour of the mystics' approach. Theirs is a particularly imaginative path. Moreover, there is a refreshing boldness in the assertion that human actions influence the attributes of God. In their approach to Halakhah, Jewish mystics clearly see themselves as more than passive respondents to the will of God; they become active participants in the ongoing cosmic drama. Mysticism brings a complex and distinctive imagery to Halakhah.

The study of Halakhah opens the door to the rich diversity of orientation which has developed within Judaism. The Halakhah itself is the overarching framework which articulates what is essential about the authentic Jewish approach to spirituality.

5 · THE SPIRITUAL JOURNEY THROUGH FESTIVALS AND PRAYER

And the Lord spoke unto Moses, saying: Speak unto the children of Israel and say to them, the appointed seasons of the Lord which you shall proclaim to be holy convocations, even these are my appointed seasons . . . (Leviticus 23:1).

Leviticus 23 presents a summary of the Jewish religious calendar. The year is punctuated by a number of festivals, each of which lends its particular quality to the Jewish way of life. Much halakhic detail is devoted to the practices associated with each festival. Such detail amplifies the intention of the biblical source and builds a complex behavioural structure around the festival. A rich variety of human emotions and strivings is thereby harnessed so that through the yearly cycle a complete spiritual renewal may be envisaged. Just as the year includes the full range of natural possibilities through the sequence of the seasons and the agricultural cycle, so the religious year addresses the range of psychological and spiritual qualities in ourselves.

But what exactly is a festival? As with so much of Judaism one needs to delve beneath the surface in order to glean something of the essential concept alluded to by the biblical and rabbinic texts. Most people today think only in terms of commemoration and celebration – a festival is merely a nudge to remember a particular event and usually an excuse for having a generally indulgent time. For Judaism, however, the festival is very much a recollection – even a reliving – rather than a memory. Ideally, it brings some historical event to life so that we can achieve in our lives what was achieved through the agency of divine intervention in the past.

In the first place, the festival is, of course, a gathering of the people – a convocation – and an important social need is thereby met. Certainly, Jewish society relishes the opportunities its festivals provide: families which may have become far-flung can reunite and friendships may be strengthened. The Hebrew root in the word for 'convocation', *kara*', intimates the spiritual purpose of the gathering, for it means 'to read aloud' and is specifically connected with reading from the Torah. The festival is the opportunity for the people to receive spiritual guidance from the word of God.

HOLY CONVOCATIONS

A somewhat deeper understanding of the import of the festivals comes from a second meaning of *kara*' – 'to happen' or 'come about by chance' (the phonetically related *karah* also has this meaning). In the rabbinic worldview an event which seems to 'just happen' by chance is generally meaningful from a higher perspective. The *mikra'ei-kodesh*, 'holy convocations', are such events. From the temporal perspective of the lower world they are days like any other – they 'just happen'. Each festival, however, represents a spiritual potency in the higher world. This potency breaks through into our lower world to infuse the day with its true meaning. The various rituals and prayers associated with the festival are the means to avail oneself of that potency.

An understanding of the true nature of the festivals is contingent on understanding Judaism's view of time. The Hebrew for 'appointed season' in the quote from Leviticus is *mo'ed*. It is related to 'ed which means both 'eternity' and 'witness'. The concept of eternity is not that of an infinite duration of ordinary passing time, but a kind of fullness of time experienced when the higher, spiritual, world is glimpsed. The word, 'ed, comprises two letters, 'ayin and dalet. 'Ayin means an 'eye' and dalet means 'door'. Eternity may occupy but a moment of passing time, but it is the moment in which one 'sees' through the 'door' of the physical world into that higher reality which sustains the physical realm. So, for example, the 'tent of meeting' where Moses encounters God is the 'ohel (tent of) mo'ed.

SACRIFICE

Leviticus 23 includes eight mikra'ei-kodesh, a complete octave consisting of different 'notes' on the spiritual scale of nourishment. Prior to this summary of the yearly cycle, the Torah states: 'When a bull, sheep or goat is born, it shall be seven days under its mother and from the eighth day and onwards it shall be acceptable as a [sacrificial] offering of fire to the Lord' (Leviticus 22:27). Why should this comment regarding sacrifice precede the discussion of festivals?

I have already referred to the symbolism of the number eight in Chapter 1. It depicts the level of transcendence, one above the natural cycle depicted by the number seven: 'The conduct of the natural world is under the number seven, since in seven days was the natural world created. Therefore whatever is transcendent to the natural world is under the number eight'.[1]

As the commentator Ibn Ezra (1089–1164) points out, the eighth day for the animal, as described in the Leviticus verse, may be compared to the eighth day for the male child, the day on which circumcision is performed. Just as circumcision completes the child, keying him into the higher, spiritual world, so too sacrifice represents the animal's elevation to the higher level. Of course, it is hard for us to countenance the view that being killed could in any way 'complete' the animal. Indeed, as we will see later in this chapter, rabbinic

76

Judaism very much sublimated the notion of sacrifice, arguing, for example, that studying the laws of sacrifice was akin to actually sacrificing the animal. Nevertheless, the message that the Torah conveys in this introduction to the festivals is valuable irrespective of our view on the whole issue of animal sacrifice.

Sacrifice is of the essence of the religious imperative. Through the yearly cycle one is enjoined to sacrifice one's lower nature and cleave to the transcendent level. Just as the animal is only 'fit' from the eighth day, so we may only achieve a foothold in the higher world through the eight mikra'ei-kodesh.

The point is further emphasized through the cryptic means that is typical of the Torah. Chapter 24, which follows the description of the festivals, begins with the command to bring 'pure beaten olive oil for the light, to cause the lamp to ascend continually'. The Hebrew for oil, shemen, is related to shemonah, meaning 'eight'. Oil symbolizes dedication to a higher purpose. It is used to anoint the king and to consecrate the priests. It fuels the light which is the primary symbol of transcendent being. Indeed, the influx from God into the transcendent sefirotic world, which sustains creation, is referred to as 'oil'. A prayer in the morning service asks that God should 'pour the good oil on the seven branches of the menorah [representing the sefirotic world] to bestow your goodness to those you have created'. Just as the lamp ascends continually by means of the oil so are we enjoined to achieve our 'ascent' by embracing the potency of the eight festivals.

PESACH, SHAVUOT AND SUKKOT

Sacred history is brought to life by the festivals. Paramount in such history is the Exodus from Egypt. The three pre-eminently seasonal festivals depict the three stages of the Exodus. First, the release from slavery and escape from the land of Egypt is encapsulated in Pesach, the season of freedom. Second, the festival of Shavuot commemorates the revelation of the Torah on Mount Sinai. Shavuot gives freedom its spiritual connotation, for in Jewish thought 'none may be considered free other than one who engages in the study of Torah'.[2] The only true freedom comes with a realization of spiritual obligations. The third seasonal festival, Sukkot, is a reminder of the wanderings in the wilderness *en route* to the 'promised land'. The observant Jew leaves the comfort of the house to dwell in a temporary structure, the *sukkah*, which is subject to the vagaries of nature. The *sukkah* is a reminder that the only real security is that proffered by the 'wings of the Shekhinah'. The roof of the *sukkah* is made of vegetation with sufficient gaps that the stars may be seen. It depicts the 'clouds of glory' which at one and the same time both conceal and reveal the presence of God.

The genius of these festivals lies in the interweaving of historical, seasonal (or agricultural), and personal aspects found in each. Pesach is at one and the same time the miraculous freeing of a people from the tyranny of bondage; the liberation of the earth as the warmth of spring brings the stirrings of new growth; and the yearning that most of us feel to escape beyond the mundane in life. Shavuot combines the historical encounter of a people with God, the season of maximum light, and the personal striving to find one's own portion in Torah. Sukkot brings a flavour of maturity: the year's fruits have been gathered and a full recognition of one's dependence on divine providence unfolds. The historical parallel is to the elevation of the people through their forty years in the wilderness so that no taint of slavery – entrapment in the mundaneness of the natural world – remained.

These distinct qualities are picked up and amplified by the choice of special readings in the festival services. Each of these three festivals is traditionally associated with a specific book of the Bible. On Pesach, the Song of Songs is read. It is understood to be a work which King Solomon wrote when he completed the Temple. Just as the Temple promotes the union of lower and upper realms, so is the Song of Songs concerned with the union between the soul and its source. It is a work full of youthful yearning for an intimate encounter with God. The rabbis understood that its verses convey the love of God for His people. The most tangible expression of this

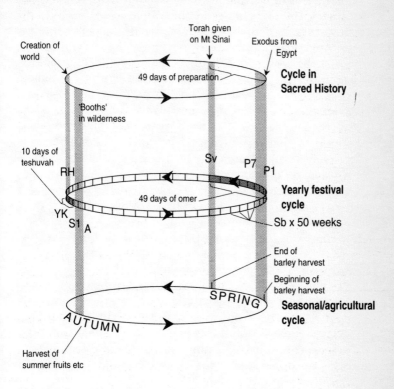

KEY

Sb Shabbat

P1 1st day Pesach

P7 7th day Pesach

Sv Shavuot

RH Rosh Hashanah

YK Yom Kippur

S1 1st day Sukkot

A Atzeret/Simchat Torah

Figure 4.   The Jewish Calendar

love came with His intervention in Egypt, the subject-matter of Pesach.

The book of Ruth is read on Shavuot. 'Your God is my God', cries Ruth, the paradigm of a whole-hearted convert to Judaism. Her story is, symbolically, the story of all who seek to renew their covenantal relationship with the Torah – the personal goal of Shavuot.

Finally, the lesson of Sukkot is conveyed in the book of Ecclesiastes. This is understood to be the work of Solomon in his old age as he reflected on the meaning of life. 'Vanity of vanities, says the preacher; vanity of vanities, all is vanity' (Ecclesiastes 1:2). The only aspect of life having real value is that which goes beyond the mundane, that which is no longer 'under the sun' in the symbolism of Ecclesiastes. As the mystics have cryptically detected, *hevel*, 'vanity', also means 'breath', the realm of the soul. *Havel havelim* ('vanity of vanities') is the rhythm of the breath – the focus of meditation – which leads us to embrace the mysteries of the soul, to explore the world 'beyond the sun'.

Here, then, is the message of Sukkot. The *sukkah* is an undeniably physical structure. Moreover, its incomplete roof of vegetation symbolizes the harvest which is representative of our seemingly endless toil in the physical world. Yet, it points to a reality which is not of this world alone. The lesson may be further emphasized by noting that Solomon's Temple was dedicated during Sukkot. The Ark and the other holy vessels were brought into the Temple,

And it came to pass, when the priests went out from the Holy Place, that the cloud [of God's presence] filled the House of the Lord and the priests were unable to stand to minister because of the cloud, for the glory of the Lord filled the House of the Lord' (1 Kings 8:10-11).

The cloud depicts the transformation of the space enclosed by the Temple. Sukkot is quintessentially about such a transformation, be it of the Temple or, on a lesser scale, of one's own personal dwelling place, the home.

ROSH HASHANAH AND YOM KIPPUR

Sukkot arrives at the culmination of an intense period of soul-searching and austerity directed towards *teshuvah*, 'repentance'. This period includes Rosh Hashanah, the New Year and anniversary of the creation of Adam and Eve, and Yom Kippur, the Day of Atonement. As we saw in the previous chapter, the whole edifice of Halakhah can be a vehicle for re-creating oneself. But it is this period of *teshuvah* which pre-eminently gives the potential for complete renewal:

> Repentance, according to the halakhic view, is an act of creation – self-creation. The severing of one's psychic identity with one's previous 'I', and the creation of a new 'I', possessor of a new consciousness, a new heart and spirit, different desires, longings, goals – this is the meaning of that repentance compounded of regret over the past and resolve for the future.[3]

It should be clear why Rosh Hashanah, in terms of sacred history, is the anniversary of the creation of humanity. We are enjoined to draw on that potency with which the Creator formed man and woman, and bend it to our own will in the endeavour to re-create ourselves. As with other festivals, the seasonal dimension blends into the spiritual intent over this period of repentance. The year, having passed summer, turns inward as the energy for growth retracts into its storage phase. Similarly, repentance demands an inward turning of psychological energy in order that our deepest nature may be scrutinized and, where necessary, remoulded for the good.

The prayers of this whole period vibrate with the themes of God's kingship and of human fallibility. The 'book of judgement' is open and worshippers 'pour out their hearts like water before the Holy One, blessed be He'.[4] But prayers are only one aspect of the work of *teshuvah*. Yom Kippur brings an added quest for purity, with its emphasis on abstinence from bodily pleasures such as food and drink. Above all, however, *teshuvah* demands a psychological commitment; a readiness to examine one's failings, and to establish the resolve with which to maintain a higher standard. As expressed by the saintly R. Kook, Chief Rabbi of British-mandated Palestine in the early part of this century: 'Teshuvah in thought precedes teshuvah in action and teshuvah in the hidden realm of the will precedes teshuvah in thought'.[5]

TESHUVAH

Teshuvah is another of those concepts which convey some-thing of the essence of Judaism. Like the Torah, it was understood to have preceded the creation of the world. This idea is bound up with a deeper understanding of creation itself. The name 'Elo'him ('God') with which the creation of the world is associated in Genesis 1, depicts God in His attribute of judgement. Hence, Rosh Hashanah – the anniversary of creation which climaxed in the creation of Adam – is also associated with judgement. Yet it was primarily in order to manifest His goodness and mercy that God created the world. In other words, the judgemental – or limiting – aspect of God is secondary to the initial divine imperative which was bountiful. The face of God depicted in Genesis 1 is concerned with setting bounds – or limits – between things in the process of creation. Teshuvah, however, is clearly associated with the initial imperative which reflects the merciful, compassionate face of God. It proffers the possibility of transcending the strict order of things and hence is considered as if it pre-dated the creation of the world.

In Jewish thought, the natural world is ruled by a certain rigidity, akin to what we would describe today as the laws of science. Teshuvah penetrates that rigidity: 'The power of teshuvah is so great that it shoots up to the Throne of Glory'.[6] Indeed, 'If a man repents it is as if he had gone up to Jerusalem, built the Temple and the altar, and offered on it all the sacrifices ordained in the Torah'.[7] The real mercy of God is seen in the potential for intercommunication which He allowed between our lower, natural world and the higher, spiritual world. Rather than leave the natural world to pursue its rigid course, as represented by the attribute of judgement, God laid a plan which included, as it were, a door between the worlds. As we have already seen, study of the Torah, and the Temple service (that is, prayer), are two of the means of operating that door; *teshuvah* is a third. The verbal root of *teshuvah* means 'to return'. Repentance is at one and the same time, a turning away from the deviations in one's path brought about by sin, and a returning to God by means of the hidden door to the higher world.

A saying in the Jerusalem Talmud conveys this idea of the transcendent function that *teshuvah* represents:

> They asked of wisdom: 'What is the punishment for one who sins?' Wisdom replied: 'Evil pursues sinners' (Proverbs 13: 21). They asked of prophecy: 'What is the punishment for one who sins?' Prophecy replied: 'The soul that sins, it shall die' (Ezekiel 18:4). They asked of the Holy One, blessed be He: 'What is the punishment for one who sins?' He replied: 'Let him repent and I shall accept him, for it is written, "Good and upright is the Lord [therefore he teaches sinners in the way)"' (Psalms 25:8).[8]

One who is wise penetrates the ways of our world, realizing that wrongdoing brings about consequences which eventually rebound on the perpetrator. Similarly with the prophet, who sees this at a deeper level in terms of the soul. Both these, however, miss the dimension which can transcend the laws of cause-and-effect, namely *teshuvah*. Judgement becomes tempered with mercy.

THE REJOICING OF TORAH

As we have seen, the festival cycle has a profound relationship to the seasons of the year. The rabbis grafted onto this primarily seasonal cycle another cycle whereby the whole Torah is read in the Synagogue in weekly portions. The two cycles intersect on the eighth day of Sukkot, known in the Bible as 'Atzeret. The last section of Deuteronomy is read together with the first of Genesis, thereby confirming that the Torah is never finished. Indeed, this reading brings the final letter of Torah, the letter *lamed*, together with the first, the letter *bet*, forming the word *lev*, 'heart'. As we have seen, for Judaism the Torah is a living organism. The lesson here is that its heart – the essence of its life – depends on its renewal. It is no ordinary book with a beginning and an end. Its end *is* its beginning.

The renewal of the Torah is a time of great rejoicing – *Simchat Torah*, the rejoicing of Torah. Thus, over a period of but a few weeks one is led through the depths of austerity and inwardness which began before Rosh Hashanah to the heights of rejoicing and abandon. Indeed, on Simchat Torah the Synagogue may appear at times more like a dance-hall than a solemn place of worship! Such a scene moved the seventeenth-century diarist, Pepys, to write:

> But Lord, to see the disorder, laughing, sporting, and no atten-
> tion, but confusion in all their service, more like Brutes than
> people knowing the true God, would make a man forswear ever
> seeing them more; and indeed, I never did see so much, or
> could have imagined there had been any religion in the whole
> world so absurdly performed as this.[9]

But whoever said that worship had to be solemn? Dancing with the Torah scroll, as encouraged on Simchat Torah, depicts the intimacy of the desired rapport between the individual and Torah. This day, 'Atzeret, is not only the eighth day of Sukkot but also the eighth of the 'holy convocations' laid out in Leviticus 23. Thus, bearing in mind what we have said already about the significance of eight, it is very much the high point of the whole cycle. The Midrash connects the name "Atzeret' with the concept of drawing near. On this day from the whole cycle, a special closeness with God may be achieved. Absolute joy is indeed the goal of this day, for joy, of all the emotions, is conducive to the experience of God.

THE EXODUS

The single most enduring feature of the sacred history of Judaism is certainly the Exodus from Egypt. In the liturgy each festival is described as 'a memorial of the Exodus from Egypt'. The Exodus is the very touchstone of the existence of the Jewish people. It conveys both a spiritual and a moral les-son. Just as God raised the people from slavery, so is the yearly cycle intended to raise a person's spiritual level. In the moral sense, the knowledge that one's ancestors suffered the rigours of slavery is intended to encourage an attitude of compassion and fairness to others. It is noteworthy that commands to treat the stranger well and to be honest in 'weights' (that is, business, see Leviticus 19:33–36) are supported by the statement that 'I am the Lord your God who brought you out of the Land of Egypt'. Similarly with the injunction against usury: 'Anyone who denies the command against usury it is as if he denied the Exodus from Egypt'.[10]

There is no creed as such in Judaism but the fundamental beliefs are very much predicated on a recollection of the Exodus. The first of the Ten Commandments states: 'I am the Lord your God who brought you out of the land of Egypt, from the house of slavery' (Exodus 20:2). Belief in God for Judaism is a belief in a God who is compassionate and who becomes involved in the events of this world. Moreover, at a more personal level, that belief is focused in the individual's potential to transcend the mundane and penetrate to the highest spiritual level. The 'you' in the verse quoted is in the singular. The statement is addressed to the individual. Whilst the historic Exodus involved a whole people, the force of the first commandment is directed to the individual Jew in the eternal present. 'Egypt' is an ever-present state. The biblical expression, 'house of slavery' itself conveys a deep lesson. A house conditions one's whole outlook; it is the base from which one goes out and to which one returns. Judaism understands that the critical point about the slavery in Egypt was not the physical hardship involved but the mental outlook of the people – an outlook ensnared in the lowest rung of mundane existence. It was for this reason that a whole generation had to pass away before entering the promised land. Physical scars are readily overcome; mental scars linger for a lifetime.

The whole story of the Exodus is laced with profound insights and pointers to the challenge we face in turning towards the spiritual in our lives. As will be evident from much that has been said already, those insights arise as one peels away the surface layers of meaning in the Torah. Let us consider just one feature of the story – the crossing of the Sea of Reeds ('Red Sea' is a mistranslation) – and examine some of its deeper implications.

The site of the Children of Israel's camp before the sea is *pi ha-chirot* (Exodus 14:9) which means 'The Mouth of Freedom'. The sea divides the realm of the Egyptians from that of the wilderness. The Hebrew for 'wilderness' is *midbar* which literally means 'from a thing (or word)'. It is the place of solitude without distractions; a place where one becomes detached from material objects and from the blabber of words. It depicts the necessary void to be traversed if one is to ascend beyond the mundane in the quest for freedom. The sea is the threshold of that void. The name of the sea, *suf* (reed), may be read as *sof* which means 'end' and is related to *saf*, 'threshold'. It is the end, or boundary, of the mundane world and threshold to what lies beyond.

Before the parting of the sea we read that the angel of God which had gone before the Children of Israel moved to their rear (Exodus 14:19). The lesson is that one cannot be led into this threshold. One may be guided up to it, but the crucial step 'into the sea' has to be made alone. This is the step into the unknown that mystics the world over emphasize. In Jewish tradition the waters divided only after the Children of Israel had entered and were up to their noses in the sea, thus emphasizing the act of faith and trust required.

The pillar of cloud, symbolizing the presence of God, comes between the Children of Israel and the Egyptians (Exodus 14:20). Here is conveyed a second lesson, this time concerning separation from impure elements. If one is to make this spiritual transition, appropriate preparations must be made to ensure that 'impure' forces are banished. 'Egypt' symbolizes such impurity. In terms that are perhaps easier to grasp today, 'Egypt' represents a restriction to the flow of energy; a 'bottling up' of potential. Holiness, on the other hand, is achieved through separation from such restrictive forces.

Furthermore, in the same verse we read that the cloud 'made light to shine in the night'. Here also is a powerful image of the spiritual challenge that the Exodus represents. Perhaps it may be useful to explore this particular image in relation to the language of contemporary psychology. Carl Jung writes that,

'It is a curious paradox that the approach to a region which seems to us the way into utter darkness should yield the light of illumination as its fruit'.[11] For Jung, this spiritual transition is achieved by penetrating the unconscious (darkness) and bringing features of its contents to consciousness (light):

> People who attempt to cross the sea without being purified and without the guidance of enlightenment [i.e., the 'Egyptians'] are drowned; they get stuck in the unconscious and suffer a spiritual death in so far as they cannot get beyond their one-sidedness. To do this they would have to be more conscious of what is unconscious to them and their age'.[12]

Successful negotiation of the Sea of Reeds entails a conquest of one-sidedness. It requires transcending one's personal pyschological orientation, as embodied in the ego, and becoming conscious of the totality of self. Such a 'journey' brings one into conscious alignment with the collective soul of humanity. The 'end' implied by the word *suf*, mentioned above, is not only the end of the Egyptian realm, it is the *end of the rulership of the body-bound ego*. The sea brings about a death of the self-centredness of personality and subsequent rebirth at a higher level.[13] The actual splitting of the sea is described in Exodus 14:21: 'And Moses stretched out his hand over the sea and the Lord caused the sea to go by means of a powerful east wind all the night, and He made the sea dry land and the waters were divided'. According to the Midrash, it was the power of the Ineffable Name of God engraved on Moses' rod which achieved these effects.[14]

The three verses which describe the movement of the angel, the shining of the cloud in the night, and the actual splitting of the sea share a distinctive feature – each consists of seventy-two letters. The *Bahir* explains how these form the secret seventy-two-letter name of God, used in spiritual exercises designed to elevate one's being. These three verses cryptically convey the real essence of the process of spiritual transformation. For the mystics, such transformation is bound up with meditative use of the Name of God.

The spiritual journey lies at the core of all religion and myth.

The story of the Exodus is the specific form this spiritual journey takes in Judaism. It also presages the eternal history of the Jewish people. As a theme of sacred history it has been recapitulated over the ages in the trials the Jews have faced in the form of dispersion and persecution. Its climax of redemption continues to be the lamp of hope which nourishes the vision of the Jewish people, a vision that unites the themes of spiritual fulfilment and world peace. The mystics, who employ complex, imaginative means to explore the personal significance of the journey, are simply adding extra emphasis to a dimension that runs like life-blood through all facets of Judaism. The journey is the central story of scripture and, as we have seen, it is spliced into time as the festival cycle of the year. It is, moreover, understood to be the foundation on which the entire body of the Halakhah is based. In addition, it occupies a pivotal place in regular prayer services.

Regarding Halakhah, the *Sifra* states that there is a relationship between the Exodus and the 'yoke of the mitzvot': 'Anyone who acknowledges the yoke of the mitzvot acknowledges the Exodus from Egypt; anyone who denies the yoke of the mitzvot denies the Exodus'. The scriptural verses to which this statement is related are particularly illuminating:

> For I am the Lord your God. You shall make yourselves holy and be holy for I am holy. You shall not contaminate your souls with any creeping creature that crawls upon the earth. For I am the Lord who raises you from the land of Egypt to be your God, and you shall be holy for I am holy (Leviticus 11:44–45).

On most instances when the Exodus is mentioned, God is described as having 'brought out' the people. Here it says He 'raises' them. The creatures that swarm on the ground represent the mundane level of existence from which one should be raised, as occurred in the passage through the Sea of Reeds. The *Sifra* understands that there is a link in the Hebrew between the words for 'raise' and 'yoke' (they share the root *'ayin lamed*). The yoke of the commandments is not viewed as a burden but as the means of separating from the lower, and cleaving to a higher, level. Indeed, maintaining separateness is the essence of holiness. On the subject of imitating God's holiness, the *Sifra* adjures: 'Just as I [God] am separate so similarly should you be separate'. Holiness is not some kind of added ingredient to be conjured out of the air; it is inherent in all things when they are maintained in their proper place. Much of Judaism is based on this important premiss.

The daily morning prayer service has been designed with the framework of the Exodus in mind. It leads one through four clearly distinct phases of prayer. At the borders between the second, third and fourth phases reference is made to the song which Moses and the Children of Israel sing on emerging from the Sea of Reeds. Just as the song in its biblical context confirms the spiritual elevation which has just taken place (see also p. 24), so in the prayer service it is intended to mark the personal elevation between the relevant phases.

THE PLACE OF PRAYER

Before examining the structure of the service in more detail, some general comments on the place of prayer in Judaism may be useful. Prayer tends to mean different things to different people: to one it is fundamentally concerned with praising God, to another it is primarily petitionary, to yet another it is for thanksgiving. There is a set order to prayer in synagogue services, but many feel that spontaneity is also crucial. The eighteenth-century Hasidic leader, R. Nachman, for example, encouraged his followers to find themselves a secluded place and pour their thoughts out to God. Others regarded such practice as unnecessary indulgence. It could well be said that all shades of opinion have found their niche within the framework of Jewish prayer and meditation.

King David wrote: 'Let my prayer be arranged before You like the incense and let the raising of my hands be like an evening sacrifice' (Psalms 141:2). The Midrash explains: 'It is as though David had said, "My Lord, as long as the Temple was standing, we arranged incense before You. Now that we have neither altar nor high priest, accept my prayer. Let the firmament open so that my prayer can come before You"'.[15] Originally, prayer was an adjunct to sacrifice but over time it came to replace it. One of the bases given in the Talmud for the institution of morning and afternoon prayer services is that they correspond to the daily offerings in the Temple. The sacrifices are, accordingly, still mentioned in the daily service. Those bringing sacrifices in Temple times were required to lay their hands on the animal before giving it to the priests, thus symbolizing the transference of their lower nature onto the animal. It is this idea of transference and elevation that becomes sublimated into prayer. The words themselves take the place of the sacrifice as the vehicle for elevation before God.

The rabbis considered Hannah to be the great exemplar of prayer: 'Now Hannah she spoke upon her heart; only her lips moved but her voice was not heard' (I Samuel 1:13). Prayer is the service of the heart, but there has to be some movement of the lips – it is not only silent contemplation. At the same time, humility is the necessary accompaniment – one's words should be inaudible to others. Intention must accompany prayer, as suggested by the term 'service of the heart' for the heart was viewed as the centre of our powers of understanding and intent. Unlike other mitzvot, a prayer offered in mechanical fashion has little merit.

One aspect of the intention and concentration cultivated in the act of praying will, of course, lie in the immediate meaning of the words of the prayer. A second concerns the general sense of being in the presence of God. Maimonides writes that a person 'should empty his mind of all other thoughts and regard himself as if he were standing before the Divine Presence'. But there is much more to intention in prayer than this alone. Here in relation to prayer, as in all other dimensions of Judaism, deeper meanings are conveyed by careful choice of words and various allusions.

THE BLESSING

The paradigmatic prayer is the berakhah, 'blessing'. 'Why does the Torah begin with the letter bet?' asks the Bahir, 'it parallels the word berakhah ... Indeed, in every place where there is bet there is a blessing, because it depicts plenitude'.[16] In the Bahir, the Torah itself is identified as a blessing. In Jewish thinking there are two dimensions to the *berakhah*. In the first place, the blessing is something which exists at a higher level but manifests in a lower sphere. It therefore gives spiritual sustenance in the lower sphere, as in the case of the Torah. Secondly, as a prayer, the blessing conveys the recognition that whatever sustenance or pleasure is derived from this lower world, it is really dependent on an influx from the higher realm, and ultimately derives from the benevolence of God. The term *berakhah* is related to *berekh* meaning a 'knee'. Even the shape of the letter *bet* is said to depict the human form bent in prayer. The blessing conveys both the metaphorical bending at the knee as the individual acknowledges the presence of the divine King and, simultaneously, the lowering from above to below of the spiritual influx aroused by such acknowledgement. A second cognate meaning of *berakhah* is *beraikhah*, meaning a 'pool' or 'spring'. By uttering the *berakhah*, the individual opens the gate to the all-cleansing divine influx which is symbolized as rain or spring water collected in a pool being drawn down in a water supply.[17]

> R. Meir says: A person is obligated to make 100 blessings each day, as it says, 'And now, O Israel, what does the Lord your God ask of you but to fear the Lord your God, to walk in all His ways and to love Him and to serve the Lord your God with all your heart and with all your soul' (Deuteronomy 10:12).[18]

R. Meir detects in this key verse from Deuteronomy a subtle hint to the centrality of making blessings. Not only does the verse consist of 100 letters but the Hebrew for 'what' gives the value of 100 through a special cipher[19] In many ways the verse from Deuteronomy is a summary of the spiritual teaching of Torah. Through the act of making blessings with clarity of purpose the full intent of the Torah is realized.

Blessings are associated with a large range of the events we experience. The observant Jew makes a blessing before eating any kind of food or drink; when appreciating a natural scene or event; when receiving good, or bad, news, and so on. Such observance engenders a deep awareness of the spiritual base underpinning our world. This is, in itself, an aim of the

Torah. In the second place, the objects or events are elevated through the *berakhah*. Food, for example, is physical nourishment; when the appropriate *berakhah* is recited, however, it becomes spiritual, as well as physical, nourishment. For Judaism, words themselves engender tangible effects in the spiritual world. The *berakhah* encapsulates the two directions of spiritual movement which are the essence of Torah. From below to above – human words raise the status of things – and from above to below – God lowers Himself to sustain the world.

Two opinions are recorded in the Talmud as to what must be included in the verbal formula to generate a valid *berakhah*. For Rav, it must include mention of the four-letter Name of God (translated as 'Lord'); for R. Yohanan, it must include mention of the Kingship of God.[20] The Talmud cryptically conveys here the deeper meaning of the *berakhah*. The purpose of the *berakhah* is precisely to bring these two dimensions together. The four-letter Name represents the transcendent nature of God – God as He is in His essence. Kingship refers to God's involvement in our world. The *berakhah* thanks God for the spiritual influx from the highest world (four-letter name) to our world (kingship).

The phrasing of the standard verbal formula used in the majority of blessings conveys further important points. 'Blessed are You, Lord our God, King of the Universe, who . . .' An example is 'who creates the fruit of the vine', relating to grapes or wine. First, note that it is God who is described as blessed. This is connected with what I have said regarding God 'lowering' Himself. Note also that the blessing includes a switch from second person ('You') to third person ('who creates'). The only direct relationship we can have with God is, perhaps paradoxically, with the transcendent nature of God. Those rare moments when intimacy with God is experienced – the mystic experience – are moments when we mysteriously slip out of the passing time associated with this, lower world, and enjoy a moment of eternity. In that moment, we know the 'Thou' that is God. By contrast, recognizing the world as a product of God's will is only an indirect experience of God. His presence in this world is concealed within the natural order and within events as they unfold through world history. The *berakhah* asks us to unify these two experiences of God, which is in fact the sublime intent of the all-embracing principle of monotheism.

MORNING SERVICE

Returning to the structure of the daily morning service, the four phases mentioned above conduct one from an initial level where God's kingship in this world is recognized and extolled, to an ultimate one where the mysteries of His essence are confronted. In outline, these four phases depict the journey to God. The first includes many blessings concerning the practicalities of life, acknowledging that all is dependent on Him. The second phase consists largely of a selection of Psalms, in which the praise of God is emphasized. This phase reflects a realization that a relationship with God is possible – praising Him is an expression of our role in this relationship. But, just as in the case of praising the work of an artist, it is an essentially distant relationship. The upper two phases of the service reveal a closer relationship. It is significant that the blessings in these latter phases change into the form, 'Blessed are You, Lord . . .', omitting the mention of God's kingship in the world. The dimension of kingship has been left behind when one enters into these upper realms.

The focus of the third phase of the service is the *shema'*, a central prayer declaring the ultimate Unity of God and all things. Beyond praise comes the realization that one is an integral part of the unity which is God. The *shema'* is fundamentally an expression of love, which epitomizes closeness to God.

The first verse of the *shema'* is the succinct declaration of monotheism: 'Hear, Oh Israel, the Lord is our God, The Lord is One'. There are many subtle allusions in this declaration, which serve as keys for a full concentration on its deepest meaning. The word 'hear' itself is significant. Sight is limited to the forward direction; hearing embraces all the six directions of space, symbolized also in the six Hebrew words of this declaration. Through hearing, those directions are unified in our consciousness, a parallel to the deeper intention of the *shema'* itself, which is to unify God's Name. Sound occupies a profound place in Judaism, reflecting the deep significance of the Hebrew language and the 'voice' of God. Moreover, there is a subtlety to hearing which can bring a poignant spiritual impact – the 'still, small voice', mentioned in I Kings 19:12, ever calls one towards union with the divine.

The three times God is mentioned in the verse allude to the biblical patriarchs: 'Lord' to Abraham, 'Our God' to Isaac, and 'the Lord is One' to Jacob. God, for Judaism, is a God of History (see Chapter 7). His unity is manifest ultimately through the events of history, a concept alluded to here since the three patriarchs symbolize the phases of Jewish history.

In the Torah scroll the last letters of the words *shema'* ('Hear') and *'echad* ('One') are deliberately enlarged. The two letters are *'ayin* and *dalet*, which we met earlier (page 76). They form the word *'ed*, 'witness' or 'eternity'. The unity of God is truly experienced when one enters that fullness of time called eternity, as discussed earlier. The *shema'* is a call to the concentration of a meditative state in which one's very being is awakened to awareness of its source.

The highest, or fourth, level in the prayer service is occupied by the silent standing prayer, known as the *shemoneh 'esreh* or *'amidah*. Prior to beginning the *'amidah*, one takes three steps forward, thereby symbolically entering the transcendent sphere where one stands directly in the presence of God. A link between the *shema'* and *shemoneh 'esreh* is achieved through the eighteen times God is mentioned in the *shema'*: the Hebrew, *shemoneh 'esreh*, means 'eighteen' and refers to the eighteen blessings it comprises.[21] The *shemoneh 'esreh* commences by blessing God for His qualities. It continues by enumerating, and blessing God for, the gifts He bestows on the individual and on the nation. And it concludes with blessings of thanksgiving.

As I have mentioned already, the immediate focus of concentration is the direct meaning of the words which comprise the body of the prayer. The words of the *shemoneh 'esreh* convey in concise and beautiful language the holiness and glory of God. Here I wish to focus on just one aspect of the deeper allusions which reveal the soul of the prayer. In this chapter I have considered the spiritual journey as it has been embedded throughout Jewish thought and practice. What relationship holds between the Exodus and the shemoneh 'esreh?

Each blessing of the shemoneh 'esreh employs the holy four-letter Name. Thus, in making eighteen blessings, we generate the seventy-two-letter name of God (4 × 18 = 72). We have seen that this Name refers to the events at the Sea of Reeds. These events, wrought by the 'Hand of God', relate to both the individual and the collective Jewish yearning to be redeemed: 'God redeemed them [from Egypt] with the fullness of His Name, the Name of the Holy One, blessed be He, with its seventy-two letters'.[22] For the individual, this is the yearning to enter the sphere of intimate rapport with God to which the shemoneh 'esreh is directed. Seventy-two is also the numerical value of the phrase 'He is, He was, and He will be'. It thus alludes to eternity which, as we have seen, is the key to this intimate relationship with God.

The Midrash states that the eighteen blessings correspond to the eighteen times the four-letter Name is mentioned (in the phrase 'as the Lord commanded' and similar phrases) in the description of the construction of the mishkan given in Exodus 39-40.[23] Again, the deeper connotation is to the intent which the worshipper should have in mind when reciting the shemoneh 'esreh. Achieving a state of closeness to God, whiich is the subline intent of this prayer, is identified with the closeness achieved through building the mishkan or Temple.

The eighteen blessings also allude to the Song of the Sea (Exodus 15:1-19). In the Torah scroll, the words of this song are arranged in the form of a ladder, or wall with interlocking bricks. As a ladder it comprises eighteen 'rungs', or lines of text down the centre column. Furthermore, the Talmud records an opinion in the name of R. Yehoshuah ben Levi that the eighteen benedictions parallel the eighteen vertebrae in the spinal column.[24] The esoteric meaning of the human body was discussed earlier in relation to the mishkan/Temple. Here, the allusion is to that which keeps humans upright, symbolically enabling our heads to reach the heavenly realm. These eighteen vertebrae form the ladder which connects the body to the head. Esoterically, the whole service involves binding and raising realms of the body, culminating in this ultimate level in which the whole is unified in the domain of the brain – the bodily 'Holy of Holies'.

On days when the Torah scroll is read in the Synagogue during the service, it is brought out from its special chamber (the Ark) following the *shemoneh 'esreh*. This, of course, parallels the Children of Israel receiving the Torah following their redemption from Egypt. It also intimates that the Torah encapsulates the divine influx descending from the highest sphere – as reached in the *shemoneh 'esreh* – down through all the levels of existence. The prayer service returns from the heights of the *shemoneh 'esreh*, bringing the worshipper finally back to this worldly realm with the assertion that the day will come when peace will reign on earth. The service thus closes with mention of the final completion of the spiritual journey – no longer personal only nor related to the Jews alone. The ultimate redemption – the messianic hope – is one to which the journey of humanity as a whole has been mysteriously directed: 'In that day the Lord will be One and His Name One' (Zechariah 14:9).

6 · JEWISH MYSTICISM

R. Yohanan says: Words of Torah only become established in one who makes himself as if he were not, as it is written, 'And wisdom is found from nothing' (Job 28:12)[1]

THE TWO PATHS TO SELF-PERFECTION

How does one make oneself 'as nothing'? We saw in Chapter 2 (p. 22ff) that humility is a prerequisite for 'receiving' Torah. One must be as a 'desert on which all trample'. Humility is a quality developed in relation to others. It begins as an outward quality but over time it inevitably influences the inner core of personality. It is a psychological fact that if one behaves in a given fashion over a prolonged period of time, the trait relating to that behaviour becomes ingrained. In this case, over time one would no longer need to practise humility; one would have become humble. Developing humility, then, represents a behavioural path of self-perfection.

There is another path which is very much the complement to this behavioural path. It is the mystical path to self-perfection. This mystical path focuses on the inner core of the person, attempting to cultivate more directly that 'nothingness' to which R. Yohanan alludes. The more one experiences oneself as comprising a core of nothingness, the more one's outer behaviour will be marked by humility. Again, a psychological principle is at work here. Those psychologists who oppose behavioural therapy argue that in order to achieve some desired form of self-change one should address the 'inner person' directly. Thus, for example, the psychoanalytic and allied approaches hold that therapy needs to gain access in some fashion to the unconscious base of personality. The mystic's goal is not dissimilar. The eighteenth-century Levi Yitzhak of Berditchev discusses a concept best translated as 'that which precedes the mind'. Daniel Matt rightly equates this concept with what we would call the preconscious in today's language. Levi Yitzhak writes: 'Thought requires the preconscious, which rouses thought to think. This preconscious cannot be grasped ... Thought is contained in letters, which are vessels, while the preconscious is beyond the letters, beyond the capacity of the vessels. This is the meaning of 'And wisdom is found from nothing' (Job 28:12).[2] Many of the practices developed within the framework of Jewish mysticism encourage a penetration of the preconscious. The mystic attempts to transcend the world of 'somethingness' which is ruled psychologically by the ego, and approach nothingness. Only in this way may one be truly open to the divine wisdom: 'One must leave intellect and mind to reach the fence of nothingness. Afterwards, "wisdom is found from nothing"', writes Levi Yitzhak's teacher, Dov Baer, the Maggid of Mezritch.[3]

The two paths may perhaps be illustrated by conceiving the individual as a circle. The circumference brings one into relationships with others and with the world of objects and events; the centre depicts one's essence. The behavioural path works at the circumference; the mystical path attacks the centre. The key point is that the entire circle is affected by either approach. Influencing the circumference changes the centre and vice versa. The use of the circle as an analogy is appropriate since there is a poignant relationship between the centre and the circumference: they may appear to be separate but neither could actually exist without the other.

THE CENTRALITY OF MYSTICISM

As we shall see, there is a great deal more to Jewish mysticism than the attempt to nullify the sense of somethingness associated with the personal ego. I have opened this chapter with these ideas to illustrate what I believe to be a crucial point, namely the centrality of mysticism to Judaism. The notion of a 'mystical' and a 'non-mystical' form of religion is foreign to Judaism. If mysticism means the attempt to draw as close as possible to God, then Judaism is necessarily mystical. The truth is that the two paths depicted above form one whole. That whole *is* Judaism. Of course, one or the other path may be closer to a given person's inclinations. Moreover, the passage of time brings about changes of fashion with the consequence that a given path is stressed more strongly in one age than in another. Nevertheless, Judaism is fundamentally about self-change and marshals both paths to this end.

In this book I have adopted an approach which has emphasized the mystical dimension in Judaism. This approach both reflects my own interests as a psychologist – for Jewish mysticism is particularly rich in its psychology – and also seems to me appropriate to the age in which we live. In our day, interest in mysticism has generally increased. Many have discerned significant points of comparison with features of modern physics and psychology. Moreover, the impetus towards direct spiritual experience, which is a hallmark of mysticism, answers a need felt by many in today's world.

Various aspects of Jewish thought illustrated in preceding chapters may be classed as mystical. As we have seen, there are mystical reasons for the mitzvot, mystical meanings in the Torah, and so on. I have attempted to show that such approaches are integral to the complex of meanings in which rabbinic thought is embedded. There is a genuine continuity between the kinds of insight conveyed by the Talmud, the Midrash and the *Zohar*, representing mainly legalistic, homiletic and mystical aspects of the Torah respectively. Many concepts which have come to be an integral part of the belief system of Orthodox Judaism were, in fact, first articulated within the mystical tradition. An illustrative example is the view that the Torah is effectively a living organism comprising levels which parallel corresponding 'levels' in organisms of flesh and blood. This view has come to be generally acknowledged within Jewish belief as a central and meaningful image of the Torah's nature, even though it stems largely from the speculations of mystics. In a famous passage, the Zohar draws a parallel of this kind between the Torah and a person. The body of the Torah is made up of the commandments; its clothing consists of the stories, which are all that may be seen by a cursory look; and its soul – 'the true foundation of the entire Torah' – is the mystical meaning discerned only through a deep encounter. [4]

Once again, the world of literal history is inappropriate to convey what is a central pillar of Judaism. Literal history dates the Zohar to thirteenth-century Spain. Moreover, its concepts and symbolism are viewed as cast in the mould of that time and place. The Zohar itself, however, ascribes its authorship to Shimon bar Yohai, a second-century master. The central pillar to which I referred concerns the continuity of the teaching that is Torah. Whilst different concepts and symbols are indeed appropriate to different ages, Orthodox belief holds that all worlds of meaning somehow inhered in the teaching which was passed down in an unbroken chain of tradition. To use another favoured image, the Torah is like a seed which gives rise to differing structures – stems, leaves, flowers, fruits – at different times. The mystical level of meaning inheres in the essence of Judaism as much as does any other aspect.

The concept of diverse levels of meaning inherent in the Torah came to be conveyed by means of a simple acrostic. The first level is that of peshat – the literal meaning. The second level, remez, refers to the allegorical meaning, particularly in the philosophical sense favoured in the mediaeval period. The third level, derash, concerns the kinds of insights advanced in the Talmud and Midrash, elucidating the text through analysis of subtle hints. It is difficult to convey the meaning of derash. The English, 'homiletic', is a dictionary meaning; but I think the term, 'mythic', is perhaps closer. Midrash is myth not in the sense of being fanciful and untrue, but in the more psychological sense of conveying something of the deeper reality lying under the surface of the narrative. It is not simply an exposition of the text, it brings the text to life by fleshing out all its complexities and nuances. The final level, sod, is the secret, or mystical, meaning which is mostly concerned with the nature of the sefirot and their interactions. The initial letters of these four Hebrew words form the word *Pardes*, Hebrew for Paradise. Thus, the fullest possible relationship with the divine – implied by the term *Pardes* – is achieved by one who embraces all levels. No one level may be downgraded by comparison with the others.

THE SEFIROT

The place of mysticism within Judaism as a whole is marked notably by its emphasis on practical experience. The Jewish mystic is primarily distinguished from his non-mystical co-religionist on account of an interest in directly exploring non-physical realities. Thus, the mystics have developed a variety of practices, both meditative and ritualistic, which lie outside normative Jewish observance. Jewish mysticism is further characterized by its fascination with the dynamics of the hidden worlds through which God's creative power unfolds. This fascination is focused on the emanations of God – the sefirot. You do not need to be a mystic, however, to speculate on creation and the nature of hidden worlds or processes. Philosophers have certainly done so over the years. What is distinctive in Jewish mysticism is the fact that the focus of such speculation – the sefirot – *are known and understood through experience* as well as through the study of Torah.

> Ten *sefirot* from nothingness. Ten and not nine; ten and not eleven. Understand with wisdom; be wise with understanding. Probe with them and explore from them. Establish a thing in its essence. And return the Creator to His rightful place.[5]

These are the words of one of the most respected works of Jewish mysticism, the *Sefer Yetzirah* (Book of Formation). Its authorship is dated by scholars around the fifth century of the Common Era. However, Jewish tradition holds that it is considerably older, viewing the patriarch Abraham as its author. The above extract conveys the importance of experience. One is required to explore, particularly in a meditative and contemplative manner, the nature of the sefirot. The interplay between wisdom and understanding refers to human faculties involved both in the study of Torah and in the grasp of reality through contemplation. Wisdom is the penetrating insight of the intellect. Discursive thought, on the other hand, is associated with understanding. Wisdom arises through the ability to clear the mind, that is, to adhere to nothingness as discussed above. If one wishes to gain insight, be it into the Torah or into outer reality (which are in fact one and the same to the Jewish mystic), one must first come to the realization that rational thought on its own is limited ('Understand with wisdom'). One must then gain the ability to enter the void, which demands initiation into meditative practice. The faculty of understanding is subsequently employed in order to grasp the insight which may have been forthcoming ('Be wise with understanding').

The primary insight of concern to the *Sefer Yetzirah* is that the world as we know it is but a covering to the world of the sefirot. The ebb and flow of nature and the multifarious appearances of things are merely manifold combinations of the inner emanations of God. The *Sefer Yetzirah* calls on one to explore this idea by using the sefirot as the measure by which things may be known ('Probe with them and explore from them'). One is able to 'establish a thing in its essence' by witnessing its inner nature – its root in the higher world. Finally, how does such endeavour 'return the Creator to His rightful place'? The term translated as Creator here is referring to God as Creator of forms (literally 'the Former'). The meditative and contemplative functions described in the *Sefer Yetzirah* are designed to uncover the inner forms of things. The striking assertion being made (and it is central to much later kabbalistic thinking) is that human consciousness itself influences God. Consciously witnessing these inner forms begins the process of returning the creative impulse back towards God. It is this process which God most desires from his human 'partners' in Creation.

The *Sefer Yetzirah* defines the sefirot as the roots of the framework that shapes our world. This framework comprises time, space, and a dimension of morality. Thus, the ten sefirot are the 'depths' of beginning, end, good, evil, and the six directions. The sefirot themselves transcend all these dimensions. They are sefirot *belimah*, sefirot 'from nothingness'. They cannot be limited by any conception of time and space: 'Their end is fixed in their beginning and their beginning is fixed in their end, like a flame bound to the burning coal'.[6]

The *Sefer Yetzirah*, in keeping with its short, cryptic tone, treats the sefirot in a highly abstract fashion. In essence, they are simply the principles that underlie the existence of ten numbers. A slight elaboration is provided by describing the first four sefirot respectively as the spirit of the Living God, air from spirit, water from air, and fire from water. It is left to later writings to draw out in more discursive fashion the qualities of the sefirot.

A central tenet of Jewish mysticism is that its fundamental ideas were present in the initial revelation of the Torah. In calling the first sefirah the 'spirit of the Living God', the *Sefer Yetzirah* alludes to Exodus 31:3 where Bezalel, fashioner of the *Mishkan*, is described as being filled with 'the spirit of God, with wisdom, with understanding, with knowledge and with all manner of workmanship'. Here is the source of the sefirot in the Torah. The first three sefirot, named in later kabbalistic literature as *keter* (crown, referred to here as the spirit of God), *hokhmah* (wisdom) and *binah* (understanding), bring into being *da'at* (knowledge). *Da'at* is not itself a separate sefirah but actualizes the next six sefirot, alluded to in the Exodus quote as 'all manner of workmanship'. These six are named in I Chronicles 29:10 as *gedulah* (greatness, also known by the name, *hesed*, lovingkindness), *gevurah* (power), *tiferet* (beauty), *netzach* (victory or eternity), *hod* (splendour), and *kol* (all in heaven and earth). The term *yesod* (foundation) rather than *kol* became the more usual designation of the ninth sefirah. The final, tenth, sefirah is included in the verse that follows. It is *mamlechah* or *malkhut* (kingdom). Figure 5 depicts the tree of the sefirot, illustrating how they are interrelated by the twenty-two paths. Each path delineates a discrete spiritual function. There are therefore twenty-two such functions, articulated through the twenty-two letters of the Hebrew alphabet. The sefirot and paths together are encapsulated in the number thirty-two which is the gematria of *lev*, heart. In Jewish mystical thought, the tree of the sefirot is indeed the very heart of creation.

The sefirot are the attributes of God. In kabbalistic thought the essence of God is the *'ain sof*, 'without end', a limitless and unknowable infinite realm. The sefirot constitute a bridge between this infinite realm and our finite world. They detail the sequence of principles whereby God's essence finds expression in the world. The Torah itself says nothing overtly about God in Himself; its concern is with God as He interacts with the world. As such, its stories and commandments may be viewed as pertaining to the sefirot.

The first sefirah is called crown since it defines the power present in the entire kingdom, that is, in the worlds that come under the influence of the sefirot (which includes our own, physical world). The crown may not act in person, but all action is contingent on the rule of the crown. *Keter* is beyond human comprehension, being merely the first, hidden, point of Will as it begins to manifest from the *'ain sof*. *Hokhmah* and *binah* were touched on above in my discussion of wisdom and understanding. A spark of an idea arising in nothingness (*hokhmah*) is given shape by *binah*. *Da'at* arises from the confluence of wisdom and understanding. It refers to knowledge arrived at through union with the object, as distinct from dualistic knowledge. *Hesed*, *gevurah*, and *tiferet* form a triad which has a moral quality. *Hesed* is the principle of expansiveness which we may experience as love. If not tempered by a limited principle of contraction – represented by *gevurah* – uncontrolled expansion would result. The interaction of these two, *hesed* and *gevurah*, generates *tiferet* as a principle of balance. Its name, translated as 'beauty', is appropriate since balance is the hallmark of beauty. The experience of beauty as a quality related to balance represents, for kabbalah, an objective truth and not simply a subjective aesthetic judgement. *Netzach* and *hod* play sustaining roles, enabling the creative impulse from above to endure in the world. This sustaining role is manifested through *yesod*, the foundation of the entire edifice. Finally, *malkhut* is the receptive principle into which the

creative impulse, having become focused in *yesod*, is finally projected.

A single name cannot, of course, convey the entire complex of features that constitutes a given sefirah. Numerous further dimensions of symbolism enliven the kabbalistic scheme. One may, for example, gain additional insight by bearing in mind that the stories of the Torah are merely outer clothing for the cryptic description of the sefirotic realm. Thus the biblical stories concerning Abraham, Isaac, Jacob and Joseph depict the sefirot of *hesed*, *gevurah*, *tiferet*, and *yesod*, respectively. Similarly, the roles played by Moses and Aaron in sustaining the integrity of the children of Israel cast light on the natures of *netzach* and *hod* respectively, to which they relate. Finally, David is the figure associated with *malkhut*. David it was who unified the kingdom and established Jerusalem as its centre, thereby preparing the ground for the Temple to be built. Indeed, it was David who brought the Ark of the Lord into Jerusalem, symbolically unifying the political and spiritual bases to his kingdom. It is this twofold aspect, the unification of otherwise divergent parts and the spiritualization of the resultant whole, which captures something of the true quality of *malkhut*. David on earth parallels the *Shekhinah* – the 'other David' as the *Zohar* puts it – in the sefirotic realm.

Further insights into the nature of the sefirot arise through a kind of spiritual anatomy, since each sefirah is traditionally associated with a specific bodily region. Thus, *hokhmah* and *binah* are the right and left sides of the brain respectively; *tiferet* is the heart; *yesod*, the genital area, and so on. In the first place, this bodily plan pertains to the primordial man, Adam Kadmon, whose form thus resonates with the whole of creation. The human form is a secondary manifestation of the entire pattern and is a vehicle for exploration of these subtle potencies. Kabbalistic practices which focus on this esoteric anatomy bear significant similarities with yogic and other techniques involving, for example, breath control, visualizations and manipulations of sound.

The sefirot depict both the creative outflow from God and the ladder of ascent whereby an individual climbs towards the absolute. These two directions of movement intersect poignantly in the relationship between *tiferet* and *malkhut*. *Yesod*, the principle which links these two sefirot, is both the channel whereby the downward creative impulse reaches its completion in *malkhut*, and the means through which the individual's spiritual work opens the way to *tiferet* and the higher reaches of the tree. The relationships between these three sefirot form a central issue in much kabbalistic literature.

UNIFICATION OF THE SEFIROT

The early kabbalistic text, the *Bahir*, discusses these relationships in a typically enigmatic fashion. It does not always use the standard names for the sefirot and actually counts them in an order different from that shown in Figure 5. Nevertheless, it serves to illustrate the issues well. *Tiferet*, counted as the sixth sefirah, is the Throne of Glory which is the sphere from which God, as King, rules the world. The seventh, *malkhut*, is viewed as the cosmic centre, balancing the opposites of fire and water and bringing peace. 'Is it really the seventh?' asks the *Bahir*. 'Is it not the sixth?'[7] In other words, is it not the role of God sitting on His Throne to bring peace? But, comes the answer, *malkhut* is the Holy Palace – the Temple – and it is the vehicle for all the other sefirot.

We have seen in Chapter 3, that the Temple is the imprint of the higher world in the lower. It is the means for the Divine Presence – the *Shekhinah* – to dwell in the world. The issue being addressed in the *Bahir* concerns the relationship from above to below. It is not enough for balance to reign in the higher realm alone. In order for the intention behind creation to be fully realized, the higher must be expressed through the lower. In sefirotic terms, *tiferet* needs to be expressed through *malkhut*; indeed *malkhut* should fully mirror *tiferet*. The two may therefore appear to be the same. Nevertheless, they express different principles and are distinct sefirot.

The *Bahir* further characterizes *malkhut* as 'thought that has no end nor object'. Here we connect with the human dimension in the mystical equation between divine manifestation and the elevation of human consciousness. The experience of such objectless thought – a state of pure consciousness – is a goal of meditative practice. We may infer from the *Bahir* that such a state aligns the mystic with the thought of God Himself: 'What did he understand that he should fear? He understood the thought of the Holy One, blessed be He.'[8] Indeed, the allusion in this discussion of pure thought is not only to *malkhut* and *tiferet*, but to *keter* also, the source of God's thought. The message of this cryptic text is that the refined state of pure consciousness plays a role similar to that of the Temple in enabling the divine to manifest in the lower world. Through the agency of human consciousness, the beginning, middle and end of the cosmic order (*keter*, *tiferet*, and *malkhut*) may become harmoniously unified.

In the graphic symbolism of the *Zohar* such unification is conveyed in overtly sexual imagery. The Shekhinah – the feminine aspect of the divine associated with the sefirah of *malkhut* – is viewed as having become separated, or exiled, from the rest of the sefirot. The desired unclouded flow of energy throughout the tree depends upon the higher sefirotic powers, focused in *tiferet*, achieving union with the Shekhinah via the intermediary of *yesod*. As the *Zohar* puts it, the King desires to be re-united with His bride. But such a re-unification of God (for the sefirot are His attributes) cannot be achieved by God alone; God is dependent on humanity. Indeed, the exile of the Shekhinah was a consequence of the sin of Adam in the first place, and the correction of this state of affairs is subsequently dependent on human conduct. Correct conduct – study of Torah and adherence to the *mitzvot* – generates the impulse from below which instigates the correct alignment of higher sefirot, that is, the union of *tiferet* and *malkhut*. The *Zohar* provides many detailed examples of how such human action is able to promote this higher union. Circumcision, which was discussed in some detail at the end of Chapter 4, is just one of many examples illustrating what is certainly a provocative conception of the mystery of God.

The foregoing is inevitably a highly curtailed treatment of the *Zohar's* 'storyline'. It is, of course, not only Jewish mysticism that employs potent sexual imagery. Mysticism is very much about the use of creative energy and it is hardly surprising that its language frequently draws on what is undeniably the paramount manifestation of such energy. But there is more to the sexual dimension than mere symbolism. Psychologically, our deepest resources are bound up with the sexual energy of the psyche. Mysticism attempts to draw on these energies and sublimate them towards its higher, spiritual aim.

MYSTIC RITUAL – THE GOLEM

This principle may be illustrated also from the more practical side of Jewish mysticism. One of the major traditions in the practical kabbalah is that of the golem. The golem is a human-like creature made through ritual means. Whilst various stories circulating from the sixteenth century onwards attest to the reality, and indeed heroic feats, of such a golem, it seems most likely that the golem was originally viewed as a purely spiritual creation. Although physical matter was used in the ritual, the activation of the golem was a spiritual, and not a physical reality. By recapitulating God's creation of Adam, the mystic was drawn into a deep encounter with the divine nature. As in many mystical techniques, the desired spiritual experience is consequent upon the powerful world of imagination being appropriately activated.

The golem ritual involves two phases. The first, in which the physical body of the golem is formed, entails what we can understand in psychological terms as an outward projection of sexual polarity. Dust from 'virgin earth' is rhythmically kneaded with 'living water' to form the clay body. The sexual energy thus activated is transformed in the second phase. Here the mystic draws on the spiritual potential inherent in the Hebrew letters as well as the power of the divine Name, in order to bring the golem to life.

This seemingly bizarre and fanciful ritual is comprehensible and indeed highly meaningful when we stress three central themes in Jewish thought. First, Judaism is rooted in *action*. Action, not contemplation or thought, is of ultimate importance. We see this principle in the Hebrew language: the roots of all words are verbs, the action words of language. As we have seen, Halakhah itself amounts to the spiritualization of the world through action. The second theme is that closeness in a spiritual sense is achieved by *resemblence*. The various religious symbols of Judaism are all based on this principle; they are physical structures which resemble higher, spiritual structures or ideas.

It is in accord with these two themes that we can understand the golem ritual as promoting a closeness to God by imitating His nature. The attempt to imitate God's nature is central to Judaism as a whole and certainly not restricted to mysticism. As discussed in Chapter 4, prescribed actions fixed in the mitzvot were specifically viewed as instilling in the individual various qualities, such as compassion, which reflected divine characteristics. The mystic goes beyond this halakhic norm by attempting to emulate God's most recondite nature, His creativity, as expressed in the pinnacle of His entire work, the creation of Adam. Just as 'the Lord God formed Adam of dust from the ground' (Genesis 2:7), so the mystic forms the body of the golem. Just as 'He breathed into his nostrils the breath of life', so the mystic 'breathes' life into the golem through the power of the Hebrew letters. Here we find the third central theme, the spiritual potency of Hebrew. For Judaism, Hebrew is a holy language. It was created by God and therefore contains an inner wisdom and spiritual power. The mystic grasps the transcendent respect in which Hebrew is held throughout Jewish literature and turns it into an experiential practice. Where the rabbis of the Midrash or Talmud may explicate a teaching based on puns in which letters are transposed or substituted, the mystics embraced the inner dynamism of Hebrew by permuting the letters, resonating their sounds and visualizing their shapes.

SOURCES OF THE GOLEM RITUAL

The talmudic source for the golem tradition already hints at this power of language. It is said that 'Rava created a man'.[9] In the original Aramaic this reads, '*Rava' bara' gavra'*', a mantra-like phrase in which the first two words permute the first two letters of the alphabet with the letter *resh*, and the third word is formed by adding the third letter of the alphabet to the preceding word.

The *Sefer Yetzirah* elaborates on the manner in which God Himself permuted the Hebrew letters in His own work of creation:

> He placed them in a circle like a wall with 231 gates. The circle oscillates back and forth . . . He permuted them, weighed them, and transformed them: *'alef* with them all and all of them with *'alef*; *bet* with them all and all of them with *bet* . . . And we find that all that is formed and all that is spoken emerges from one Name.[10]

The exact nature of these permutations has engaged many minds and filled numerous manuscripts. 231 is mentioned since it is the number of two letter permutations from the Hebrew alphabet of twenty-one letters, without including reversals. Another tradition holds the number of 'gates' to be 221.

Permuting Hebrew letters in a meditative state is not limited to the golem tradition. It features in many mystical practices, for example those directed towards attaining the prophetic state – an inspired state of consciousness. The Hebrew word meaning 'to permute', *tzeruf*, also means 'to refine' and 'to join'. To the mystic, permuting Hebrew letters effects a refining of oneself and a joining to God since they are the very agents of His ongoing creativity. With regard to the golem in particular, letters bear specific bodily references and are used therefore to enliven corresponding limbs in the golem. Thus, for example, in the *Sefer Yetzirah*, *bet* corresponds to the mouth, *gimel* to the right eye, *dalet* to the left eye, and so on (although, again, diverse traditions are found).

In Genesis 12:5 it is stated that Abraham 'made souls in Haran', which the mystics understood as referring to his 'golem-making' activities. In their eyes, Abraham became the paradigm of the succesful adept in this mystic practice. Because such golem-making represents the noblest imitation of God's own creative powers, Abraham merited an intimate encounter with God. This is expressed in some versions of the *Sefer Yetzirah* in which, after asserting that Abraham was 'successful in creation' in relation to the 'soul-making' in Haran, it states that:

> Immediately there was revealed to him the Master of all, may His Name be blessed forever. He placed him in his bosom and kissed him on his head and called him, 'Abraham my beloved' (Isaiah 41:8) ... He made with him a covenant between the ten fingers of his hands – this is the covenant of the tongue – and the ten toes of the feet – this is the covenant of circumcision.[11]

The kiss represents true closeness to God. Further, the role of creativity as being the key to this closeness is intimated in the second half of the extract. As mentioned in Chapter 4, the two covenants symbolically express the two faces of human creativity, the first being intellectual (the tongue, that is, language) and the second, physical (circumcision, that is, sexuality).

The manner in which these two faces are integrated in the golem ritual may be illustrated by citing one of the classic 'recipes', that of R. Eleazar of Worms (12th – 13th century). In his commentary on the *Sefer Yetzirah* he writes of one who would make a golem that

> It is incumbent upon him to take virgin soil from a place in the mountains where no one has plowed. And he shall knead the dust with living water, and he shall make a body [golem] and shall begin to permutate the alphabets of 221 gates, each limb separately, each limb with the corresponding letter mentioned in *Sefer Yetzirah* ... And always, the letter of the [divine] name with them.[12]

The inclusion of the divine Name introduces a seal of transcendence into the operation. The holy four-letter Name of God undoubtedly defines the heart of Jewish mysticism. Jewish mysticism is paramountly a mysticism of language, and paramount in the Hebrew with which it spins its web of ideas is the holy Name. Through the long history of Jewish mysticism whole worlds of meaning and intricate meditative systems have been attached to the letters of this Name. In addition, the existence of further esoteric names, for example, the seventy-two-letter name discussed in Chapter 5, adds to the rich complexity of name mysticism. Indeed, the twelfth-century Spanish exegete, Nahmanides, articulates a central premise when he writes in the introduction to his commentary on the Torah, that the entire Torah is composed of the Names of God, if we could but discern it. Overtly, the text of the Torah has been divided into words conveying historical stories and the commandments of God. However, at Mount Sinai Moses was also given the Oral Tradition, according to which the Torah may be read as a sequence of Names. Judaism regards a Name of God not simply as an appellation, but as a set of letters and/or numbers which precisely depict one or more of His attributes. Exploring the mystery of a Name is tantamount to exploring God directly.

The golem ritual conjures up a dark and mysterious chapter in which magic fuses with spiritual intent. Yet, as I have suggested, it emerges as a credible, albeit mystical, expression of mainstream Jewish belief and practice. As a creative expression of religious belief, it even resonates with a number of peculiarly 'modern' issues. In its involvement with earth and water it accords with the ecological imperative to be in touch with nature. In a psychological sense, the golem represents the union of opposites (male and female, matter and spirit) which Jung saw as instrumental in the process of individuation. It thus accords with the psychological imperative to know one's self. Indeed, the whole ritual may be thought of in modern terms as an endeavour to re-create oneself in the limitless image of God. Finally, it articulates a view of God as attainable, as a presence with whom one may express a shared creativity. The golem ritual indeed embodies an especially rich integration of the three-fold partnership of humanity, nature and God, for which religions seem to be searching today.

And yet it is a dark myth. The spiritual being created in the holy ritual has become the all-powerful monster set loose by some crazed scientist. The myth is corrupt. Why?

The answer to this question is complex. It involves the change in outlook brought on by the machine age whereby we have become estranged from natural forces and even intimidated by our own creativity. It involves also the shift to dualistic thinking, associated with Descartes' philosophy, which encouraged us to view the body as a kind of machine, independent of mind. But the seeds of corruption go back further still. The myth became corrupt when people began to consider the golem as some kind of real (that is, external) creature. Stories of this nature were already circulating in the sixteenth century. Prior to this, Jewish texts emphasized the inner, or at least non-physical, nature of the ritual.

Perhaps it is not possible to suggest a single reason for the loss of that outlook which allowed the golem ritual to be spiritually uplifting. A complex of historical and cultural changes sealed the golem in its tomb. However, there is one factor that stands out as playing an important role in its demise, namely anti-semitism. From the Jewish point of view, the wish to enlist the aid of a powerful, real creature to protect the community from Christian-inspired attack underlies much of the later golem mythology. In other words, the golem became less of an end in itself and more of a means to an end. Originally, creating a golem was in itself a spiritual goal. Indeed, the notion that the golem should enjoy any kind of prolonged existence independent of the adept, was foreign to most early texts. From the sixteenth century onwards, however, the golem increasingly became a means to achieve a worldly goal, as in the example of protection.

But more damaging still was the manner in which the golem became a vehicle for the most powerful features of the feared yet despised image of Jews in Christian eyes. The Jews had 'killed God'; yet here they attempted to bring dead matter to life. The Jews were considered to be in league with the devil, possessing the dark secrets of mystic creation. Indeed, the major charges laid by Christianity at the feet of Jews over the centuries all revolved around the mysteries of life itself and the symbolism of resurrection: the blood libels, the killing of Christian children, desecrating the host, poisoning wells. The Christian myth of the Jew thrived on the idea that Jews could devilishly make life from matter. Moreover, the life thus created was – like the Jews themselves – inordinately powerful. Predating the myths of superman and the sorcerer's apprentice was the myth of the golem that is able to draw on hidden reserves of power and may, occasionally, run amok. Finally, the golem was not quite complete – in most texts it is portrayed as lacking the power of speech. This was like Judaism itself in Christian eyes: born of a deep encounter with God, but now blind to the 'new covenant'.

No other image strikes so directly at the heart of the tension between Christianity and Judaism. The myth of the golem trembles with the weight it had to bear. For it lay in the shadow of the absolute central image of Christianity – that of God incarnate and the resurrection. The golem was something that Christians could not quite understand, yet instinctively feared. So too with Judaism itself – its continuity defied the very logic of Christianity, and the Jews became the victims of probably the most powerful irrational fears the world has known.

These statements need not be restricted only to the particular instance of the golem. The history of Judaism became inextricably linked to the effects of anti-semitism. As we turn to look at Judaism today and at its possible development in the future, this tension between Christianity and Judaism needs further examination. For only through deep insight into the past can we hope to lay the ground for a wholesome future . . .

7 · THE SILVER CORD

> Remember now your Creator in the days of your youth . . .
> while the silver cord be not yet loosed, nor the golden bowl
> shattered, the pitcher broken at the foundation nor the wheel
> severed at the pool (Ecclesiastes 12:1-6)

The final chapter of Ecclesiastes is a many-layered plea to
uphold spiritual values over all else in life. The 'silver cord'
is interpreted in the Midrash in two complementary ways. On
one level the imagery in the chapter depicts the decay of a
body, the silver cord referring to the spinal cord. The other
interpretation sees the silver cord as the unbroken cord of
tradition spanning the generations. The two images easily
come together when we realize that the deeper meaning
is to the Torah – and indeed Judaism itself – as a living
being. The life of this mystical being is dependent on the
spiritual work of individuals. But a degree of collectivity and
continuity is essential. Any organism is of necessity a whole
that is greater than the sum of its parts. And the organism's
life clearly expresses its continuity over time. In the imagery
of Ecclesiastes, it is the silver cord which maintains the coher-
ence of the Jewish people as a collective body. Just as the spinal
cord unifies the disparate parts of a body in space, so the cord
of tradition unifies over time.

Tradition. The word practically pulsates with the image of
Judaism in many eyes. There can be no doubting the power

of tradition to unite a people, and Judaism, with its peculiar history of being on the receiving end of untold oppression, undoubtedly owes its survival in large measure to the richness of its traditions. But tradition alone is not enough. There has to be recognition also of the realities of the age in which one lives. Any age throws up its share of ephemeral fashions, and a religion such as Judaism rightly resists any pressure to shift from its high ground. But there are also more fundamental changes beneath the surface of society. For a religion to survive it needs to detect and respond to those deeper currents which carve out the landscape of history.

There exists a necessary tension between the desire to adhere to the old and the need to adapt to the new. Over the ages various inspired individuals have recognized the deeper historical currents and have instigated appropriate change in Judaism. A classic example is that of R. Yohanan ben Zakkai who 'negotiated' with the Romans at the time of their conquest of Jerusalem. He was permitted to leave Jerusalem and join other sages at Yavneh, some thirty miles away. He built up the rabbinic academy there, enabling it to take over the mantle of leadership from Jerusalem. The geography itself was only symbolic of the major shift that was wrought through the work of ben Zakkai and his circle. Power shifted from the centralized priesthood to the more devolved rabbinic, or Pharisaic, tradition. In many ways the changes necessary to enable Judaism to survive the destruction of its Temple in 70 CE had already begun to unfold. Ben Zakkai marshalled these changes and projected Judaism forward in its metamorphosed guise. Crucially, the sense of continuity was strongly emphasized. For example, in fixing the order of prayers, ben Zakkai's circle established connection not only with the sacrificial service but also with the biblical tradition. It was understood that Abraham, Isaac and Jacob had instituted the morning, afternoon and evening services respectively. Similarly with the Halakhah: as we have seen, the continuity of halakhic authority was viewed as stretching back to Moses at Sinai.

The ideological revolution wrought by the rabbis of this period has carried Judaism through the best part of two thousand years. Of course, over such a long period of history Judaism did not remain a monolithic culture. Geographic dispersion gave rise to many varieties of practice. Nevertheless, these were largely accommodated within the fundamental rabbinic framework. In the wake of the eighteenth-century enlightenment and subsequent Jewish emancipation, however, fundamental ideological issues became challenged.

The map of Judaism today largely reflects those challenges. The various Non-Orthodox movements (for example, Reform and Conservative Judaism) view the Halakhah as an essentially human response to social and historical, as well as spiritual, forces. For these movements, the notion that the Oral Torah and, in particular, the Halakhah represent a line of continuity reaching back to Sinai proved untenable. It could not be squared with the rationalistic flavour of enlightenment thinking, and these movements have departed substantially from halakhic tradition. A significant schism has resulted, with Orthodox Judaism unable to accept the premises on which such departures were made. Orthodox Judaism holds firm to the notion of the divine origin of Halakhah and the concomitant concept of an unbroken line of teaching from Moses through the rabbis of the Talmud and ultimately to modern rabbinic authorities. Even Orthodox Judaism, however, has been moulded in certain important ways by enlightenment thinking and emancipation. It was not only Reform Judaism, for example, that integrated within itself features of the philosophical outlook and religious mores of the dominant Christian culture.

There are many books which detail the differences in practice across the contemporary Jewish spectrum. My discussion of modern Judaism in this last chapter will focus on what I see as being the more substantial currents in the broad sweep of history which will shape Judaism over the near future. As will become clear, the seeds of these currents lie in the time of Yohanan ben Zakkai and his fellows. They involve the split which took place amidst the ashes of Judaism's Temple culture. Rabbinic Judaism represents one side of this split; what became Christianity represents the other. The birth of Christianity cast a shadow over Judaism which has not only wrought great suffering. It has also subtly influenced the very meaning of what a religion is, which inevitably impinged on Judaism's own outlook. There are two events of our day which I believe to represent the beginnings of the final resolution of that split. They are the two events which, by any analysis, have generated more change in Judaism within a period of fifty years than have any events over the last nineteen hundred. I refer to the Holocaust and the establishment of the State of Israel.

REVELATION THROUGH HISTORY

In this short book I have tried to convey the major tenets of Judaism. I come now to what may be considered the most poignant of these, particularly in relation to modern history. It is the belief in revelation through history. For Judaism, not only is God present in history, but the very essence of His revelation to humankind is contained in the historical process itself. History bears a transcendent meaning. A truly 'Jewish' response to the Holocaust can, therefore, never be satisfied with the view that it was only the consequences of human action. The hand of God, albeit at some remove, hovered above the death camps of Europe.

The Hebrew Bible itself chronicles the notion of revelation through history. Its stories are not simply moral or allegorical. They convey what it is that God wishes us to know about Himself. For Judaism, the major biblical characters are, at one and the same time, both historically real and also characterizations of the attributes of God. Abraham is, for example, not only a character who displayed certain laudable attributes; he is the vehicle through which God manifests His lovingkindness (hesed) in the world.

The Hebrew Bible cryptically indicates that the very Name of God was revealed through history. A close reading reveals a significant parallel between the numbers of the early generations and the numerical values of the letters of the Name (yod = 10, heh = 5, vav = 6, heh = 5). From Adam to Noah included ten generations – the yod of the Name. Five further generations reach to Peleg – the heh. The root of Peleg literally means 'to divide'. It is understood that his was the generation in which the world was divided – due to the events of Babel. The deeper meaning is that it is at this point in the sequence that the Name is divided, the first two letters being somewhat separated from the last two. The third letter of the Name – *vav* – takes the sequence through six more generations to Isaac, and the group from Jacob to Moses includes five generations, making up the final *heh*. The most profound meaning of the story of the Exodus is bound up with this actualization of the Name through Moses. As it says, 'And God spoke to Moses and said to him, I am YHVH. I appeared to Abraham, to Isaac, and to Jacob by [the different name of] 'El Shaddai, but by my Name YHVH I was not known to them' (Exodus 6:2-3).

We have seen that the festivals also commemorate this idea of revelation through history. Each festival draws on a particular spiritual potency which came into being through a certain divine act in the world. Of particular interest to post-biblical history are the events celebrated in the festival of Purim. Purim recalls the saving of the Jews from an attempt to destroy them, as depicted in the book of Esther. And by extension, it is a celebration of the survival of the Jews despite numerous outbreaks of anti-Jewish hatred over the centuries.

The relevance of the book of Esther to post-biblical history lies not only in its subject matter but also in the picture it paints of God's involvement in history. The name of God is conspicuously absent from the book. 'Where is there an allusion to Esther in the Torah?' asks the Talmud.[1] 'In the expression, "I will surely hide My face" (Deuteronomy 31:18)', comes the answer, drawing on the similarity in the Hebrew between 'Astir (I will hide) and 'Ester. This comment ingeniously conveys a central feature of the book of Esther, for God's face *is* hidden in its action. Events unfold through what could be called coincidences: the king just happens to owe the Jewish hero a favour; it just happens that he could not sleep on a crucial night, etc. Indeed, the very name 'Purim' means 'lots', for in the story lots are cast for the villain to decide on which day to destroy the Jews. Of course, coincidences and acts of fate are to be viewed as far from random – the hand of fate is none other than the hand of God.

It so happens that I am writing these words on 10 November 1992. Last night was the anniversary of Kristallnacht which has come to mark the symbolic beginning of the Holocaust. Hundreds of synagogues and Jewish premises in Germany were destroyed. According to the *Encyclopedia Judaica*, at least 30,000 Jews were arrested to be sent to concentration camps, thirty-six Jews were killed and thirty-six seriously injured. There is an uncanny turn of fate in the fact that it is also the anniversary of the fall of the Berlin Wall. To Judaism, historical events are implicitly symbolic, their structure being contingent on God's directing hand.

There are several issues in the modern world – ecology, the role of women, for example – to which Judaism must respond. I will come to these. No issue, however, looms so large as does the Holocaust. It is hard to understand how so much destruction was wreaked on so defenceless a minority in the heart of 'civilized' Europe. The fact is that one can only begin to understand it from the vantage point of history. The Holocaust forces us to examine the meaning of history.

It is not simply a case of Judaism picking itself up after a fall. In the fullness of time, the Holocaust will surely be seen as a marker of the culmination of one cycle and the beginning of another. Whilst the Holocaust sealed the fate of one source of creativity within Judaism, namely the significant centres of Europe, so the establishment of the State of Israel opened another. In certain respects, it is a new kind of Jew who has arisen from the ashes of Auschwitz.

The enormity of the Holocaust defies one's credulity. If any of my readers doubt this, then let them look elsewhere. There is no shortage of testimony. My interests as a psychologist lie in the underpinnings of the nightmare. The Holocaust achieved its horrendous scale on account of the way in which the Nazis were able to graft twentieth-century technology onto an ancient prejudice. The anti-semitism which developed in the breeding ground of Christian Europe and made the Holocaust possible, bears the hallmarks of collective psychopathology. Many writers have developed this theme. To my mind there can be no doubt that the virulent nature of the Christian accusations against Jews, some of which I mentioned at the end of the previous chapter, demands an explanation in psychological terms.

JUDAISM AND CHRISTIANITY

The roots of an explanation lie in the foment within Judaism around the time of the birth of Jesus. It was clearly a time of upheaval. The culmination of this upheaval as far as spiritual practice is concerned was the destruction of the Temple. In order to survive the upheaval, what had been a highly centralized, sacrifice-based religious culture had already been transformed into a more decentralized prayer-based culture. As we have seen, what became Judaism as we know it today arose through this transformation. Prayer became a sublimation of sacrifice and the Halakhah emphasized that the physical and the spiritual realms may be united in principle without the need of a Temple. The intricate detail of everyday life became the field through which spirituality interpenetrated physicality.

What became Christianity took a very different path. The events of Jesus' life became infused with a meaning which directly opposed the Pharisaic (that is, rabbinic) outlook. One can readily see that the notion of the incarnation of God and the death of Jesus carried the principle of sacrifice into a new age. But it did so by distancing mere mortals from the interpenetration of spirit and matter. Christianity rejected the spiritual value of bodily action. Spirit and matter were irreconcilably divided. This dualistic principle – which had been largely a Hellenistic import through the hand of Paul – became the seed for a forceful rejection of the body.

Christianity was a rejection of Judaism. The vehemence of its rhetoric against the Pharisees helped it to mark out its own territory. It made the Pharisees into something they never were, however, for it failed to understand the spiritual value in Halakhah. The more other-worldly Christianity became, the more it feared the worldliness of the Jew. The caricature of the Jew promulgated since the Middle Ages placed him in the dark corners, in the shadows, in the heart of gross physicality. He gloried in money, the key to this-worldly success, and conspired to control and manipulate the strings of worldly power. These, and more, were fantasies projected by the dominant religion onto the Jewish minority.

In a psychological sense, that which we reject about ourselves festers in the unconscious. In Jung's model of the psyche, for example, it becomes the 'shadow' which is projected outwards onto those around one. In the normal course of development, an individual generates an idealized image of their self. Since falling short of this ego-ideal is inevitable, one of two possibilities must ensue. If the ego-ideal is not modified then the shadow becomes ever more powerful and dangerous. The other possibility represents the path of psychological growth. The individual recognizes their own limitations and begins to integrate the contents of the shadow. This is the first stage of the process of individuation whereby the individual achieves a sense of wholeness in relation to the self.

It would seem that Christianity promulgated an ideal which was unrealistic, certainly for the vast majority of its adherents. Total rejection of the spiritual value attaching to matter in general, and the body in particular, could never be fully integrated within the psyches of its practitioners. Equally, the clarion cry to 'Love thine enemies' itself became divorced from the path Christianity took over the centuries. In short, the ideals of Christianity, valuable perhaps to a band of outsiders in a time of upheaval, could never sit easily in the world of power with which Christianity became synonymous.

Christianity needed a scapegoat. In the beginning it rejected its 'parent' religion, and, as it became all-powerful in Europe, so it projected its shadow onto the scapegoat it had created.

Many psychologists have stressed the impact in the Christian psyche of the Jews being seen as the 'killers of God'.[2] This image undoubtedly powered much psychopathic behaviour. But why were the Jews cast in that role in the first place? The real battle was between the two differing worldviews: Jewish monism which, as argued above, upheld the union of spirit and matter, and Christian dualism which split them asunder. Monotheism is the bedrock of Jewish belief. The rabbis emphasized again and again that all was ultimately One. Indeed, the words on the lips of countless Jewish martyrs as they died at the hands of their persecutors were, poignantly, those of the *shema'* – the Lord is One.

The crisis of belief today is bound up with the predominantly dualistic outlook. The issues that will carry us into the next millennium are, I am sure, those which accompany a return to monism. It is a paradox indeed that those who espouse a return to holistic spiritual values in relation, for example, to ecology, often tar Judaism with the brush which they use to tar Christianity. How often do we hear that the 'Judaeo-Christian' heritage distances us from spirituality in nature? Judaism does not distance us from nature. Indeed, there is no such thing as the 'Judaeo-Christian' heritage. As I have indicated, Judaism and Christianity are literally poles apart. What has distanced us from nature is the dualism promulgated through the Christian heritage, and through the ages of enlightenment and industrialization which rode on its back.

These latter factors have, of course, significantly influenced Jewish culture. If we wish to pursue an ecologically-sensitive spirituality, it is people and their attitudes we need to change. Judaism itself, with its celebration of the seasons through its festivals, for example, will not be found lacking. Indeed, many aspects of Jewish teaching project a profound respect for the natural world. There is, for example, a New Year specifically for trees. Moreover, there are features of Jewish law which afford trees in particular special protection. The way of Halakhah represents spiritual ecology at its most sublime, for it brings a mature recognition of the religious value of human involvement with the natural world. It resists the tendency – all too apparent around us today – towards a weak, sentimental attachment to nature. More importantly, it promotes the celebration of the natural world without empowering the forces of paganism. There is a world of difference between an approach which elevates and ultimately unites natural forces by seeing them as the symbolic handiwork of the One God, and one which worships the intrinsic power of those forces themselves. Again, it is the Nazi period which should be called as witness to exemplify the dangers of paganism in the modern world. But that would certainly take us too far afield . . .

The point of this highly summarized psychological excursion into history has been to enable me to address contemporary issues in a clearer focus. There are certainly many examples where anti-semitic images still linger in western society. In the wake of the Holocaust, however, the Christian shadow has undoubtedly begun to be checked. No longer, for example, are Jews officially held to be 'collectively responsible' for Jesus' death. Whether Christianity will fully integrate its shadow is a question for others to consider. But Jews generally no longer bear the full weight of others' psychopathic projections. Judaism has largely been freed from the restrictive sense of being defined in relation to something else, namely Christianity. Moreover, the primary symbol of freedom – one's own State – has become a reality. As the Israeli national anthem puts it, 'The hope of two thousand years – to be a free people in our land, the land of Zion and Jerusalem'. The establishment of Israel has breathed a spirit of renewal into Judaism which will undoubtedly have far-reaching and creative effects.

THE STATE OF ISRAEL

In talmudic and midrashic literature, Jerusalem is portrayed as the centre of the world. When we consider the cultural and political map today it almost seems that this portrayal has come of age. Israel is not merely a tiny strip of land; it is one of the most powerful archetypal ideas the world has known. It is pre-eminently the archetype of wholeness and integration. The name, Israel, first appears in the biblical story of Jacob wrestling all night with the angel of God. When he prevails over the angel he is told that his name will be changed, 'since you have struggled with God and with men and have prevailed' (Genesis 32:29). This name-change symbolizes the highest level of integration. Jacob becomes Israel when he begins to realize his unique destiny; when he has successfully negotiated the spiritual journey through darkness. The Genesis passage precedes Jacob's daytime encounter with his feared brother, Esau. There is a profound lesson here, for one may come to terms with the outward, physical embodiment of one's fears only when one has integrated their inner, psycho-spiritual core. Jacob's journey is one which Judaism as a collective being has made more than once, but never more poignantly than in our day.

Two thousand years of prayers directed towards the restoration of 'Zion' have carved a niche in the heart of every Jew. Israel is a tangible, external witness to the continuity of a spiritual dream. This is not to suppress the significance of the political and territorial problems associated with the State of Israel. Indeed, the very responsibility that accompanies the power of statehood has introduced an element not known in Judaism throughout those two thousand years. If there were a need for Judaism to come to terms with such responsibility, that region of the globe certainly provides a poignant testing ground!

THE VISION OF JUDAISM

The existence of Israel is totally bound up with what I see as the major challenge facing Judaism today. Judaism must renew itself through contact with its central sources. It must assert its own authentic vision which has actually become tarnished, or at least covered over, with the dualistic heresy nurtured in Christian Europe. This is an assertion only possible by a people no longer cowed by subservience.

In asserting this vision, however, Judaism must not be merely backward looking. As I have tried to show, the rabbinic worldview stresses a strong form of holism. The world of modern science is itself today emphasizing the holistic principles which seem to govern the natural world (ecology), the world of matter (physics) and the mind (psychology). Judaism is very much an intellectual discipline. It seeks to delve into the hidden nature of things. Its attitude to Torah parallels the scientific outlook on reality. The notion of religion as something compartmentalized off from scientific enquiry, something related to the realm of spirit alone, is itself a product of the dualistic heresy. There is indeed a fruitful rapport between Judaism and science which may be expected to grow.

But, of course, religion is fundamentally about belief and practice. The question of belief goes to the heart of the dualistic heresy. We make a great mistake when we attempt to isolate belief. A belief is not something that can be assessed as some kind of abstract premise, or even proved by some erudite philosophical argument. When examined from outside the whole context of the religion, any belief will inevitably be found wanting. The notion that the entire Oral Torah was passed from God to Moses is such a belief. The meaning and worth of this belief is bound up with the whole edifice of teaching which is Judaism. The ability of a belief to stand up to rational logic is of secondary importance, for the primary value of the belief lies in its ability to open the individual to that spiritual realm in which chance becomes meaning and time becomes eternity. Faith is like the oil which allows the great wheels to turn.

WOMEN IN JUDAISM

Many of the issues of concern in our day revolve around the nature of practice, in particular as far as women are concerned. A typical Orthodox prayer service, for example, is a highly male-oriented affair. Issues bound up with feminism are not purely of passing fashion and many feel that Judaism must integrate within itself a richer role for women. Judaism has often been portrayed as strongly patriarchal. This reputation is not generally deserved, although there are elements of Jewish law and practice which are restrictive towards women. The rules concerning divorce in Orthodox Judaism, for example, make it impossible for a woman to divorce her husband against his wishes. There are currently strong voices for such laws to be emended.

In Chapter 1, I emphasized the role of the home in Jewish life. Traditional Jewish practice places a woman's role largely within the context of her centrality to the home. It is the woman, for example, who lights candles in the home to usher in the ambience of Shabbat and festivals. And all the many mitzvot and customs concerning food and family life are primarily her responsibility. Nevertheless, prayer and

Torah study are just as much means for women to express their spiritual aspirations as they are for men. Indeed, there are famous instances of learned and respected female figures throughout Jewish history; Deborah in the Bible and Beruria in the Talmud are two examples. However, it is in relation to the religious life of the home and education of children that Jewish women have traditionally found their major niche. The critical question today concerns our responses to changing cultural and social circumstances.

Clearly, the amount of time and energy a woman needs to devote to the home is very much less today than in, say, talmudic times. Moreover, rigid male–female demarcations are less pronounced. A woman may have an active secular life which precludes the kind of domestic role traditionally conjured up. She may be the major earner in a family, or she may have decided not to marry. To what extent are the religious roles assigned to men and women in Judaism merely conditioned by the socio-cultural environment of past ages? In answering this question quite fundamental matters come to the fore. These extend beyond the immediate question of female spiritual practice, and concern Judaism's attitude to issues of principle and, more generally, the nature of the role that religion plays in contemporary life.

At the outset a distinction must be made between Orthodox and non-Orthodox traditions. Non-Orthodox traditions have no difficulty in adapting to contemporary attitudes and generally reject practices which entail any differentiation between male and female religious roles. Thus, in Reform or Conservative Judaism women may take a fully active role in all Jewish practice, even filling the traditionally male-only role of rabbi.

Orthodox Judaism has a very different approach to issues of principle. There are two kinds of principle involved here. One is basically philosophical and psychological: it concerns the essential qualities of maleness and femaleness, and the ways in which each should be expressed in religious life. The second principle is to do with the Halakhah: what generic rules governed Jewish practice as established in previous times? It is this second approach which defines Orthodox Judaism.

For Orthodox Judaism, the philosophical and psychological ideas are too vague and subject to the whims of fashion to be allowed to dictate religious practice. The central tenet, which applies in all spheres and not only here in relation to women's religious roles, is that *the earlier the source, the closer to God's revelation and therefore the more authoritative is its statement*. We may arrive at an understanding of philosophical or psychological principles only through rational analysis of the consistent patterns in biblical and rabbinic sources and in the writings of later, authoritative commentators.

To take a specific example relating to gender roles, the Talmud establishes that communal prayers, as well as certain responsive portions of the prayer service, may only be recited when there is a quorum of ten men present, a *minyan*. Since there is no ambiguity in the statement that the *minyan* must be composed of men, Orthodoxy could not countenance the inclusion of women in a *minyan* today. (Of course, women may pray at the same service as their menfolk – although separation is maintained. The point here is more technical, concerning as it does the nature of the *minyan*.) In considering this talmudic ruling, the first and crucial point to make is that any suggestion that the Talmud is simply articulating a view conditioned by its cultural milieu is antithetical to Orthodox understanding. Halakhic precepts are seen as transcending such factors. Indeed, if this were not the case, the Talmud's fundamental authority would necessarily evaporate. The appropriate approach here is to establish the principles on which this ruling about the *minyan* is based. In brief, these principles concern the difference between public and private prayer. For Judaism, there is an injunction on men but not on women to engage in public religious activity (prayer services, Torah readings etc.). Were this attributable only to the idea that women did not have time – on account of domestic responsibilities – to be committed to regular, public services, then today, when many women would have time, they should be subject to an injunction (and would therefore be equivalent to men in the *minyan*). A careful reading of sources indicates that such was not the reason.

The reason for these kinds of distinctions between male and

female religious practice is more deeply connected with what 'public' and 'private' represent. The Midrash makes the point that the rib, from which woman was created in the biblical story, is an inward part; it is not visible from the outside. For Judaism, the female nature is inward, and therefore private. A woman's potential is connected with her sexual role of enclosing, or taking within. (The Hebrew *'aizer* ('help'), used to describe woman in relation to man in Genesis 2:20 is cognate to *'azarah* ('enclosure').) Religious expressions as formulated in Jewish sources are all connected with this potential. Thus, for example, a woman is obligated to pray and study privately. This does not necessarily mean on her own socially, but in a private capacity religiously. Thus, today many Orthodox Jewish women gather in groups for prayer and/or study. Such a group may encourage a sense of shared, and thereby enriched, spiritual experience. In 'technical' terms, however, the prayer in such groups is private in nature, not requiring a *minyan*. Men, on the other hand, again in synchrony with their sexual role, achieve their potential through outward projection of activity. Their primary religious role is accordingly outward, or public. These rulings are predicated on the premise, central to Orthodox Jewish thought, that a person's true nature and potential is interrelated with their sexual nature. Of course, all this is specific to religious activity and is of no consequence as far as secular occupations are concerned.

For Orthodox Judaism, these fundamental orientations of man and woman can never change and, accordingly, the orientations of their respective religious roles should not change. There is no value judgement intrinsic to these roles. If any comparisons between male and female spirituality (as distinct from religious roles) may be made on the basis of Jewish sources, it would be in the direction that women have a more refined spiritual nature than men. Men are subjected to a larger number of *mitzvot* than women, not because these give men greater access to higher spiritual realms, but because men intrinsically need more discipline against which to hone their natures.

This brings us to perhaps the most fundamental question: what is the place of religion in our lives? The real challenge that feminism lays at the door of Judaism, and indeed of religion in general, transcends the particularities of gender roles. It concerns the manner in which the religious 'instinct' finds expression in different ages.

Our day has seen a shift in religious matters which parallels the general shift in society. As society has become more materialistic so people's attitudes to religion have become determined by analogous 'material' considerations. Obviously, to many, materialism is equated with the death of religious belief – the material world is all there is. I am not concerned here with this extreme position; my concern is with those who maintain some sense of the value of religion. The shift to which I referred comprises two aspects. Firstly, there is a kind of consumerism about religions whereby one is able, even encouraged, to assess the goods on offer, as it were. One may even pick and choose from within a religion. The yardstick for making such choices is ultimately down to the individual's personal experience. And here lies the second, and in the context of this discussion most important, shift in religious aspirations. There is a general view current today which holds that religion is essentially about the having of experiences. Spiritual experience tends to be seen as the primary commodity that religion offers. This attitude is quite foreign to classical religious, including Jewish, sources.

To the extent that spiritual experience is inward and private it relates more to the feminine than to the masculine capacity, as described above. This emphasis on spiritual experience cannot be lightly dismissed. I believe that it represents a deep and fundamental shift in people's orientation to matters religious in the broadest sense. It is interesting to note in this context that kabbalistic sources from many centuries ago predicted a shift towards the feminine in the run up to the days of the Messiah. It is stated that originally in creation the sun and moon (symbolically male and female respectively) were of equal strength. Only later did the moon become diminished in scale. In the days of the Messiah the moon will regain its former glory and shine with its own light. Symbolically, the Shekhinah – God's feminine aspect, will guide the world towards ultimate peace and harmony. Or, to put it another way in kabbalistic terms, *malkhut* will assert its status as the completion of the entire tree of sefirot.

Returning to the immediate aspirations of Jewish women, the perception that more profound spiritual experience is associated with the roles traditionally assigned to men is an illusion. Judaism is not traditionally configured around the desire to 'have' spiritual experiences. Even within Jewish mysticism, the path which focuses on experience has tended to be the minority path. Jewish mysticism has often been more concerned with the deepest meaning of the Torah than with the cultivation of experiential states. Judaism is structured primarily around the concept of fulfilling obligations, or mitzvot. An individual, male or female, who undertakes a mitzvah to which they are not strictly subject is not seen as achieving any special merit. Judaism, through Halakhah, lays a ground plan to our lives which harnesses male and female spiritual potential to the higher design as portrayed in God's revelation. Ultimately, one's potential is realized through the ideal unit which includes both male and female – namely the home. The man is fulfilled through his wife's embracing of the female religious role, as is the woman through her husband's actualization of the male role. Such fulfilment may have absolutely nothing to do with whether either, or both, parties experience some kind of spiritual uplift through their actions.

The challenge for Judaism today is not simply that the family as an institution is under threat. The challenge fundamentally concerns the shift towards the more inward dimensions of religion. Simply grafting women into roles traditionally exclusively male does not address this issue. An individual woman may find some fulfilment as a Reform rabbi, but is no closer to spiritual experience merely through occupancy of that public office than is a male rabbi. The real shift that Judaism is beginning to embrace is away from the supremacy of 'public' ritual and prayer and towards their more 'private' aspects. This, I believe, is where the significance of feminism lies.

The outer face of Orthodox Jewish practice will be maintained on the basis of traditional male–female roles. Of this I have no doubt. The principles on which these roles are established are fundamental to everything Judaism stands for. The notion of the male as active and giving, and the female as private and receiving is central to Jewish understanding of God and His relationships to the world and to humanity. It is also inherent in practically the whole corpus of halakhic and kabbalistic thought. One cannot abandon these principles and hope to hold onto a meaningful, 'updated' religion. They penetrate Judaism's very heart. And, moreover, I believe that they are grounded in a solid perception of human nature.

The inner face of Judaism is another matter entirely. Whereas in the past, it was only an élite that desired actively to explore the spiritual world through mystical means, today, under the influence of those shifts that go hand-in-hand with feminism, large numbers are so motivated. Whereas in the past it was only those who were strongly grounded in rabbinic learning, today those who quest for spiritual experience include many who do not have a learned foundation. Whereas in the past it was uniquely men who sought the numinous, today gender is irrelevant.

We are witnessing today a shift from Judaism's outer face towards its inner face. Traditional roles become a springboard to deeper exploration of our spirituality. Whether a woman or a man feels limited within a traditional Jewish religious role is more a question of their level of understanding and of the opportunities available for active spiritual work than of the role itself. It is the need for such active exploration on a broad scale that is important. Traditionally, the path to practical experience opened by the mystics has been hemmed in with limitations of one form or another. Today, the path should be more accessible to both men and women. Teachers are needed who recognize the scope and potential dangers of such psycho-spiritual exploration but do not rely solely on the safety net of talmudic learning. Such teachers should include women. There is a related need today to break down the somewhat monolithic congregational structures which were the hallmark of diaspora Judaism. In fact, the role of rabbi as congregational leader was always problematical. The rabbis of the Talmud largely frowned on the notion of a 'career rabbi'. It is interesting to note that Maimonides, for example, trained as a physician specifically to avoid the need to support himself through his rabbinical work. In Israel, much more informal – yet Orthodox – approaches are becoming the norm. There are significant moves today towards smaller, informal groups generally, and I feel sure that these will increase. They can fulfil a need which is felt by many men as well as by women. Such groups may not be motivated necessarily towards mysticism, being perhaps more concerned with prayer and study. But their orientation towards personal experience, in line with the shift I have discussed, will mark them as being characteristically 'modern'. Moreover, women's groups will continue to explore expressions of feminine spirituality in ways that are surely new. What is the difference, for example, between lighting candles as a routine and lighting them as the climax to a meditation on the feminine quality of the Shekhinah? How – to take another example – might the celebration of the New Moon be infused with an awareness of female sexual and spiritual power?

These kinds of questions rapidly shade into the mystical domain, and it is to Jewish mysticism that both women and men seeking a more active sense of the spiritual in their lives are increasingly turning. Certainly, the restriction on women becoming involved in mysticism is no longer appropriate and, for many, has already begun to disappear.

THE FUTURE

And here perhaps lies the crux of Judaism's immediate future. Jewish mysticism comprises a core of revealed truth which is held to have been maintained throughout Judaism's long history. But those truths are carried by means of a framework, a myth of the age. Today, a new myth is awaited. Our myth will surely place emphasis on the role of that which is feminine in the psyche of humankind, an emphasis perhaps on the intuitive ability of the mind to bind together diverse images. It may be, for example, that the Shekhinah will no longer be seen as passively awaiting her consort but rather as more actively orchestrating the circumstances through which she may reach her fulfilment. The myth will, furthermore, give meaning to the sacrifice of those who died in the Holocaust and to the arising, phoenix-like, of Israel as a spur to religious renewal. A comment of Rashi on the very opening of the Torah will also play its part. The comment itself appears in the Midrash Yalkut to Exodus 12:2. But Rashi, writing in France at a time when rulership of the Holy Land was being fought over by Moslems and Christians, cryptically places it at the head of his commentary. The comment argues that God is the arbiter of land ownership and that the Jews' claim to the land of Israel is validated by biblical authority. But of what relevance is such authority unless the world accepts it? It seems that Rashi perceived a higher significance in the world-wide dissemination of the Bible through the auspices of Christianity.

The last renewal to have become fully integrated within the Jewish world was that emanating from the Israeli mountain town of Sfat in the sixteenth century. The circle of mystics who made Sfat their home included both a powerful visionary, Isaac Luria, and a gifted systematizer of ideas, Moses Cordevero. But the birth and success of the Lurianic vision was not attributable to individual personalities alone. A variety of key factors came together around that time. The first of these factors was the cataclysmic expulsion of the Jews from Spain in 1492. The resulting migrations led to the circumstances in which the Sfat circle of mystics came together in the mid-sixteenth century. Moreover, the enormity of the catastrophe in Spain very much implanted in the Jewish consciousness the need for renewal. The second factor contributing to the creative generation of ideas in Sfat was the transition to a relatively secure period for the Jews of this area under Ottoman rule beginning in 1517. There were also equally significant factors of a more global nature, not unique to the Jews. A general spirit of renewal – the spirit of the Renaissance – was abroad. The great age of discovery had set the expansive horizons of the day. The impetus to chart new territory in an intellectual and artistic sense was spurred by those who had set out into the unknown by ship. It seems hardly coincidental that the New World itself was discovered, as far as this European spirit was concerned, in 1492. Finally, the spread of the new kabbalistic vision through the Jewish world owed much to the growth of printing. The first Hebrew book had been published in 1475 and the sixteenth century saw an explosive impact of printing on the intellectual world.

There are significant parallels to each of these factors today. The cataclysm of Spain has been re-enacted, in yet more powerful form, in the Holocaust. The transition to a 'golden period' of Ottoman rule is a pale precursor to the establishment of self-rule in the Jewish State. I believe it is not fanciful to equate the expansive climate triggered by the age of geographic discovery to that in our own day triggered by the exploration of space. And finally, the information technology revolution is having an impact on the dissemination of ideas which parallels that of printing in the fifteenth and sixteenth century.

All the limbs would seem to be in place. We await only the power of the imagination which may breathe renewed life into them.

> Then He said to me: 'Prophesy to the spirit. Prophesy, O son of Adam, and say to the spirit, Thus says the Lord God: From the four directions come, spirit, and breathe into these slaughtered ones that they may live' (Ezekiel 37:9).

> R. Yehudah says: 'It was truth – a parable'. R. Nechamiah said to him: 'If true, why a parable, and if a parable, why the truth?' Rather, [he means to say] *by means of* truth, it was a parable.[3]

> *It was a parable.* Because it was a hint to them that the exile is like a man. Just as he will return to life, so Israel will return from exile.[4]

APPENDIX: THE HEBREW ALPHABET AND THE NAME OF GOD

The Mishnah ('*Avot* 5:6) presents a list of items that were created by God at twilight preceding the first Shabbat. Examples include the manna which fell in the desert, the rainbow used by God as a sign to Noah after the flood, and the mouth of Balaam's ass which miraculously spoke. All of these represent entities that transcend the natural order of things. The Mishnah intimates that their miraculous potential was stored up for their rightful time. One item in the list continues to bear witness to the transcendent – the script of the Hebrew alphabet. As Rabbeinu Yonah writes in his commentary, the reference here is to the miraculous letters of the Torah written in 'black fire on white fire'. But even the pale reflection of these fiery letters – the Hebrew alphabet as written – is viewed as containing something of the higher wisdom. For Judaism, the Hebrew letters are sparks of the highest divine world; they convey something of that transcendent reality into the finite world in which we live. The Mishnah hints at a principle which becomes most fully elaborated in the mystical tradition, in which complex meanings are read from every nuance of the letters and many meditations are based on their forms and permutations. This idea that a higher meaning inheres in the alphabet and language underlies the depiction of Hebrew as the 'Holy Tongue'.

The divine origin of the letters is symbolically implied by the slight curl at the top left of each letter. This curl represents the origin of the letter י (yod). The י is the only letter which does not extend fully down to the writing line. It stands for that which is always 'above' the physical world. The Talmud (Shabbat 104a) offers the insight that י stands for ירושה (yerushah), 'inheritance'. The inheritance is the Torah, itself symbolized by the number ten (Ten Commandments) which is the numerical value of י. The י is the transcendent source made manifest; the divine inspiration in both the Hebrew letter and the spiritual teaching. It further intimates activation, for the Hebrew יד (yad) – cognate to the name of the letter – means 'hand', symbolically that which enables the will to be expressed. This point is also conveyed by means of the rules of Hebrew grammar. The י is used for the male (third person singular) imperfect verbal form. Its 'maleness' points to its initiatory role, for in classical Jewish thinking, the male is the instigator of action.

The letter י opens the four-letter Name of God, יהוה. Its topmost point represents the primary manifestation of something out of nothingness, with the rest of the letter depicting the initial impetus of the creative Will. The second letter is ה (heh) which functions to enable that impetus to be sustained. The letter ה depicts the feminine. Again, this idea is conveyed clearly by the rules of Hebrew grammar. ה generally denotes the feminine, both in noun and verb forms. It is also the definite article, further hinting at its symbolism for in sustaining the creative impetus it enables something definite to come into being. The feminine gives shape, or definition, to the male impulse.

Kabbalistically, the first ה of the Name represents the sefirah of binah which receives the creative influx from hokhmah. The union of these two generates the third letter of the Name, ו (vav). In shape the ו is effectively a י which has been extended to the writing line. It depicts the development of Will through the subsequent six sefirot (the numerical value of ו being six).

It denotes linkage, the word וו (vav) meaning a 'hook' and the letter itself being used as the conjunctive 'and'. It represents the desire of the initial expression of the divine nature in the י and the ה to reach its fullest manifestation through being linked, or united, with the final expression of divinity in the final ה of the Name. This final ה represents the Shekhinah, the female aspect of God which conveys the divine nature into the world.

It can be seen from the foregoing that the Name of God depicts the creative process itself. The essence of God is conveyed in His Name as a process. This is apparent also in the fact that the Name derives from a verbal root, היה (hayah), 'to be' or 'become'. Being, in Jewish thought, is not a state but a process. God is that process of becoming which underlies all reality. This process of becoming is most incisively approached through the paradoxical relationship between revealing and concealing which defines the nature of Torah in its widest sense. Involvement in Torah study and in the world of Halakhah therefore brings one into the very heart of that process of becoming in which God's revelation is one and the same as God's essence itself.

The letters of God's Name share certain properties. In the first place, unlike all the other letters, they denote vowel sounds. Unlike consonants, vowels are elongated by the breath. The breath, as carrier of pure sound, is our most direct contact with the divine process of becoming itself. Second, again uniquely in the alphabet, these letters combine with the Hebrew ל (lamed) and ב (bet), which are the two letters in the word לב (lev), 'heart'. (The combinations arise in the forms of the two letters as prepositions meaning 'to' and 'in'.) The letters of the Name thus carry a poignant relationship to the heart. Both of these ideas become keys to many meditations in which awareness of the heart and breath plays a central role.

The gematria of the Name is twenty-six which hints at the first letter of the alphabet, א ('alef), since the א comprises three component strokes: a sloping ו (vav, value 6), with a י (yod, value 10) above and an inverted י below it. The א is a silent letter, symbolizing the silence that precedes manifest action (symbolized in turn by the explosive 'b' sound of the second letter, ‏ב‎ – bet). Again, the letters convey a lesson strongly picked up in the mystical tradition, namely that God is pre-eminently found through silence.

The ‏א‎ is, moreover, the principle of balance. It depicts the harmony achieved through the very creative process alluded to in the Name itself. The upper ‏י‎ is the transcendent source giving of itself. The lower ‏י‎ is in position to receive the influx as it is equilibrated through the agency of the ‏ו‎. This is the harmony of creation desired by the Creator – that the human hand should receive what is bestowed from the divine hand and reflect the gift back, illuminated by the light of consciousness. In its symbolism the ‏א‎ is mirrored by the six-pointed Star of David which comprises two triangles. The upward-pointing triangle symbolizes the impulse from below which elicits the higher impulse symbolized by the downward-pointing triangle. The fire of human spiritual endeavour is answered by the rain of divine influence. In the star, the two are in perfect balance, hinting at the idealized kingdom of David, through which a harmonious alignment of heavenly and earthly powers will be achieved.

Letter	Name	pronunciation and transliteration*	Meaning	Numerical value	Significant associations
א	alef	silent, '	learn/ox	1	Silent letter; balance; also means 1000
ב	bet	b, v	house	2	Explosive beginning ('b'); duality; giving kindness
ג	gimel	g	camel/wean	3	Third completes a cycle; giving kindness
ד	dalet	d	door	4	Door to expansiveness; four directions
ה	heh	h	the	5	Used by God to create this world
ו	vav	v	hook	6	Six directions; conjunction; extended י
ז	zayin	z	weapon	7	Centre of six; sustenance; cyclical time
ח	chet	ch as in 'loch', h	cord	8	Transcendent to space/time; octave
ט	tet	t	clay	9	Physical matter open to higher design
י	yod	y	hand	10	Hand that moulds the clay; direction
כ	kaf	k, kh	palm	20	Weigh in hand; כ means 'as' or 'like'
ל	lamed	l	learn	30	ל extends above; spiritual teaching
מ	mem	m	water	40	Purification and renewal; consciousness

Table of the Hebrew alphabet, indicating the symbolism of each letter

* These rules of transliteration have not been applied in cases where Hebrew words are commonly used in anglicized forms.

Letter	Name	pronunciation and transliteration*	Meaning	Numerical value	Significant associations
נ	nun	n	flourish	50	Gates of understanding; jubilee
ס	samech	s	support	60	Circular letter; God as place of world
ע	ayin	silent, '	eye	70	Insight; perceiving unity in diversity
פ	peh	p, f	mouth	80	Language; gives expression to insight of ע
צ	tzadi	tz	righteousness	90	Also means 'hook'; draws person higher
ק	kuf	k, q	monkey	100	Holiness; alludes to 100 daily blessings
ר	resh	r	head	200	Inheritance; also wicked ('headstrong')
ש	shin	sh, s	tooth	300	Grinding; cyclical process; threefoldness
ת	tav	t	mark	400	Impression in physicality; boundary; seal

Table of the Hebrew alphabet, indicating the symbolism of each letter (continued)

* These rules of transliteration have not been applied in cases where Hebrew words are commonly used in anglicized froms.

NOTES

Chapter 1. An Outline of Jewish Belief and Practice

1. Mishnah, '*Avot* 1: 2.
2. B. T. *Yoma* 39a.

Chapter 2. Torah: The Essence of Judaism

1. *Song of Songs Rabbah* 1:2.
2. B.T. *Menahot* 43b.
3. B.T. *Nedarim* 32a. 'Covenant' is interpreted here to mean the Torah.
4. B.T. *Shabbat* 88a.
5. Genesis Rabbah 1:1.
6. *Midrash Tanhuma* (Buber) ki-tisa.
7. B.T. *Hagiga* 3b.
8. Mishnah '*Avot* 5:25.
9. B.T. *Nedarim* 55a.
10. B.T. *Ta'anit* 7a.
11. Cited in M. Idel, *Kabbalah: New Perspectives*, Yale University Press, 1988, p.190.
12. The authority of the Oral Torah has been questioned more than once in Judaism's history. For example, the Karaites, a sect originating in the eighth century claimed that the rabbinical tradition as found in the Talmud and other works deflected Jews from the essential revelation of Torah. In more modern times the various factions within Judaism differ largely according to their attitudes to the authority of the Oral Torah.

Chapter 3. Shabbat and Temple

1. B.T. *Shabbat* 49b.
2. B.T. *Berakhot* 55a.
3. *Pesikta Rabbati* 6:6.
4. Midrash Tanhuma, *Pekudey* 3.
5. Note the parallel phrasing in this verse describing the completion of the Mishkan to that used in both the completion of the Temple by Solomon and the completion of the six days of creation, quoted earlier.
6. *Sefer Yetzirah* 1:1.
7. Cited in R. Patai, *Man and Temple*, Thomas Nelson & Sons, 1947, p.114.
8. Mishnah '*Avot* 3:21.
9. The letter *bet* is generally sounded as 'v' when it is in the middle or at the end of a word.

Chapter 4. Halakhah: The Way of Holiness

1. B.T. *Sotah* 14*a*.
2. *Sifra* on Leviticus 19:18.
3. B.T. *Berakhot* 8*a*.
4. Genesis Rabbah 9: 1.
5. B.T. *Shabbat* 88*b*-89*a*.
6. J.B. Soloveitchik, *Halakhic Man*, Jewish Publication Society of America, 1983, p.46.
7. B.T. *Bava Metzi'ah* 59*b*.
8. Midrash Tanhuma, *Tavo* 1.
9. J.B. Soloveitchik, *op. cit.* ,p.109.
10. B.T. *Sanhedrin* 21*b*. The second command to which R. Yitzhak refers – not to multiply horses – was similarly broken by Solomon.
11. B.T. *Makkot* 23*b*.
12. Cited in M. Idel, *op. cit.*, pp.184–5.
13. *Zohar* I, 98*b*.
14. *Zohar* III, 142*a*.
15. E.R. Wolfson, 'Circumcision, vision of God, and textual interpretation: from midrashic trope to mystical symbol', in *History of Religions*, *27*, 189–215, 1987.

Chapter 5. The Spiritual Journey through Festivals and Prayer

1. R. Judah Loew (Maharal of Prague), *Ner Mitzvah*.
2. Mishnah 'Avot 6:2.
3. J.B. Soloveitchik, *op. cit.*, p. 110.
4. Midrash on Psalms 119:76.
5. A.I. Kook, The Lights of *Teshuvah*, transl. Ben Zion Bokser, *Abraham Isaac Kook*, SPCK, 1979, p.123.
6. *Pesikta de Rav Kahana* 24: 12.
7. Leviticus Rabbah 7: 2.
8. Jerusalem Talmud, *Makkot* 2:7, 31*d*.
9. R. Latham, *The Shorter Pepys*, Bell & Human, 1985, p.313.
10. *Sifra* on Leviticus 25:37–38.
11. C.G. Jung, Collected Works, vol.11, *Psychology and Religion: West and East*, 2nd ed., Routledge & Kegan Paul, 1969, p.508.
12. C.G. Jung, Collected Works, vol.14, *Mysterium Coniunctionis*, 2nd ed., Routledge & Kegan Paul, 1970, p.200.
13. I have explored the psychological approach to the theme of light in darkness, and related spiritual issues, more fully elsewhere. See B. Lancaster, *Mind, Brain and Human Potential: the Quest for an Understanding of Self*, Element Books, 1991.
14. Midrash on Psalms 114:9.
15. Midrash on Psalms 141:2.
16. Bahir 3–5.
17. Genesis Rabbah 39:11.
18. B.T. *Menahot* 43*b*.
19. The cipher involves substituting the reverse orders of letters: *tav*

for *'alef, shin* for *bet* etc. In this case the Hebrew for 'what' is *mah*. Substituting *yod* for *mem*, and *tzade* for *heh* yields a numerical value of 100.
20. B.T. *Berakhot* 40b.
21. Although an additional blessing was inserted, making nineteen in total, this has not deflected rabbinical thinking from the deep significance of the original number.
22. *Pesikta Rabbati* 15:17.
23. Midrash on Psalms 29:2.
24. B.T. *Berakhot* 28b. In actual fact there are twenty-four vertebrae in the column. The 'error' does not, however, deflect from the symbolic intent of the statement.

Chapter 6. Jewish Mysticism

1. B.T. *Sotah* 21b. The quote from Job is (as ever) ambiguous. It is normally translated as 'From *where* may wisdom be found?' However, the Hebrew *ma'ayin* can mean 'from nothing' as well as 'from where'.
2. Cited in D.C. Matt '*Ayin*: The concept of nothingness in Jewish mysticism, in R.K.C. Forman (ed.) *The Problem of Pure Consciousness*, Oxford University Press, 1990, pp.140–1.
3. Cited in Matt, *op. cit., p.140.*
4. *Zohar* III, 152a.
5. *Sefer Yetzirah* 1:4.
6. *Sefer Yetzirah* 1:7.
7. *Bahir* 154.
8. *Bahir* 79.
9. B.T. *Sanhedrin* 65b.
10. *Sefer Yetzirah* 2:4-5.
11. *Sefer Yetzirah* 6:7.
12. Cited in M. Idel, *Golem: Jewish Magical and Mystical Traditions of the Artificial Anthropoid*, State University of New York Press, 1990, p.56.

Chapter 7. The Silver Cord

1. B.T. *Hullin* 139b.
2. Most scholars would agree that the New Testament's version of events, portraying the Jews as responsible for Jesus' death cannot be accurate. It was a myth which was instituted, and subsequently propagated, for polemical purposes. Even as recently as 1981, however, a typical children's school-book could write that 'Jewish leaders . . . hanged him [Jesus] on a cross, like a common criminal' (*Read and Respond*. Book Three). That such inflammatory material should be directed at impressionable children is truly inexcusable.
3. B.T. *Sanhedrin* 92b.
4. Rashi's comment on the *Sanhedrin* passage.

GLOSSARY OF HEBREW
TERMS AND NAMES

(All dates CE unless BCE is stated.)

'Aggadah   Non-halakhic teaching material in rabbinic literature; comprises stories, ethical teachings and interpretations of biblical texts.

'Amidah   The standing, silent prayer; also known as *shemoneh esreh*, a name alluding to its original 18 blessings.

The Bahir   A major work of early kabbalah; first circulated at the end of the 12th century in Provence; authorship attributed to R. Nehuniah ben Ha-Kana of 1st century.

Berakhah   'Blessing'.

Joseph Caro   (1488-1575); expelled from Spain and Portugal; lived in Turkey then Israel; mystic and halakhic authority; author of the *Shulchan 'Arukh*, a major code of Halakhah.

Gematria   Interpretation of sacred text based on numerical values of letters.

Havdalah   Ceremony to mark the end of Shabbat or festival.

Halakhah   Jewish law; discussions and rulings concerning the exact practical details involved in performance of mitzvot.

Hebrew Bible   Canonized sacred texts, including *Torah*, books of the Prophets and other writings such as Psalms and Proverbs.

Kabbalah   Literally 'receiving'; term for Jewish mysticism, especially as formulated from 12th century onwards.

Kiddush   Ceremony of sanctification used at commencement of Shabbat and festivals.

Maimonides   R. Moshe ben Maimon (1135-1204); born in Spain but persecutions forced flight, first to Morocco then to Egypt where he became physician to the Vizier of Saladin as well as leader of the Jewish community; major philosopher and codifier of *Halakhah*.

Mezuzah   Container attached to door-posts in house; contains parchment scroll with words from the *Torah* (portions of the *shema'*).

Midrash   Corpus of homiletic rabbinic literature; classical **midrashim** extend until the end of 10th century; also term for whole genre of interpretation based on allusions in the text.

146

Mishkan The Tabernacle described in book of Exodus; forerunner of the Temple in Jerusalem.

Mishnah Earliest rabbinic codification and record of the Oral Tradition; written c.200 under editorship of R. Yehudah Ha-Nasi in Israel; records halakhic rulings and much detail of the religious practice during the preceding age.

Mitzvah (pl. **mitzvot**). A religious command prescribed in the *Torah*; details of mitzvot are preserved through the Oral Tradition.

Pesach Passover; spring festival celebrating freedom from slavery in Egypt.

Purim Festival celebrating the saving of the Jews from the first recorded attempt at genocide – that intended by Haman, as recorded in Book of Esther.

Rabbi Teacher; one learned in Torah; abbreviated as R.

Rabbinic Judaism Judaism as formulated by the rabbis mainly of the talmudic period; the term largely refers to Jewish learning and practice as taught by those who wished to preserve the continuity of the Oral Tradition: 'Moses received Torah from Sinai; he handed it down to Joshua; Joshua to the elders; the elders to the prophets; and the prophets handed it down to the men of the Great Assembly' [which ruled c.500-300 BCE] (Mishnah, 'Avot 1:1); to all intents and purposes **Rabbinic Judaism** means Orthodox Judaism as understood today.

Rashi R. Shlomo ben Yitzhak (1040–1105, France); wrote extensive and authoritative commentaries on most books of the Hebrew Bible and Babylonian Talmud; his biblical commentary emphasizes both literal and midrashic interpretations.

Rosh Hashanah Jewish New Year.

Sefer Yetzirah Early mystical text, attributed to the patriarch Abraham; concerned with the nature of Hebrew letters as agents of creation.

Sefirah (pl. **sefirot**) An emanation of God; the term designates a complex amalgam of the principles of number and meaning; the ten **sefirot** form the central glyph of kabbalah, the tree of life.

Shabbat Sabbath; day of holiness and rest as a reminder of God's work of creation; begins before sunset on Friday and extends until three stars are visible on Saturday night.

Shavuot Festival recollecting the revelation of Torah on Mt. Sinai.

Shekhinah The indwelling presence of God. In kabbalah, the

Shekhinah is understood as a feminine aspect of God identified with the sefirah *malkhut*.

Shema' A central prayer declaring the unity of God; focuses on the love of God and the dependence of earthly matters on divine providence; comprises Deuteronomy 6:4-9 & 11:13–21 and Numbers 15:37–41.

Shemoneh 'esreh See *amidah*.

Simchat Torah 'Rejoicing of the Torah'; festival marking the end and the beginning of the weekly Torah reading cycle.

Sifra Rabbinic, halakhic commentary on the book of Leviticus.

Sifre Rabbinic, halakhic commentary on the books of Numbers and Deuteronomy.

Sukkot Autumn festival recollecting the journey through the wilderness; commemorated by dwelling in a temporary structure, the **sukkah**.

Talmud The **Babylonian Talmud** (referred to as B.T. in the notes) comprises the Mishnah as well as the Gemara which records the discussions on the Mishnah in rabbinic academies of Babylon up to the end of the 5th century; the **Jerusalem Talmud** was edited in Israel a century earlier; the Talmud is the major work of rabbinic Judaism, comprising the roots of all subsequent halakhic rulings as well as much aggadic material.

Targum Aramaic translation of the Bible; most important is **Targum Onkelos** (2nd century) which incorporates significant interpretations, as well as the literal translation, of the original Hebrew.

Tefillin Ritual boxes containing scrolls with extracts from the Torah; worn on upper arm and head during morning prayers; symbolize the dedication of action (arm) and intellect (head) in divine service.

Teshuvah 'Repentance'.

Throne of Glory The essence of the world of creation (a higher world in kabbalistic thought) from where the divine influence is directed into the lower worlds.

Torah Spiritual teaching revealed from God to Moses; the term conveys more than simply the 'five books of Moses' (**Written Torah**) since it includes also the entire oral tradition which elucidates them (**Oral Torah**).

Yom Kippur Day of Atonement.

The Zohar The major text of kabbalah; attributed to the 2nd century rabbi Shimon bar Yohai; modern scholarship considers its final author to be Moses de Leon, 13th-century Spain.

Selected Further Reading
(English Only)

GENERAL

Hebrew Bible, (King James or RSV versions).

Encyclopaedia Judaica. Keter, 1972.

Authorised Daily Prayer Book (Singer's), 3rd rev. ed., 1990.

Baron, S. W.   *A Social and Religious History of the Jews* (18 vols.), 2nd. ed. Columbia University Press, 1952–80.

Berkovitz, E.   *Not in Heaven: The Nature and Function of Halakhah*, Ktav, 1983.

Carmi, T.   *The Penguin Book of Hebrew Verse*, Penguin, 1981.

Cohn, N.   *Warrant for Genocide: The Myth of the Jewish World-Conspiracy and the Protocols of the Elders of Zion*, Penguin, 1969.

Dawidowicz, L.   *The War Against the Jews*, Penguin, 1977.

Gilbert, M.   *Jewish History Atlas*, 3rd. ed., Weidenfeld & Nicolson, 1985.

Green, A. (ed.)   *Jewish Spirituality* (2 vols.), Crossroad, 1986–9.

Munk, E.   *The World of Prayer* (2 vols.), Feldheim, 1961–3.

Roth, C.   *A Short History of the Jewish People*, Horovitz, 1948.

Steinsaltz, A.   *Biblical Images: Men and Women of the Book*, Basic Books, 1986.

Wistrich, R.   *Anti-Semitism: The Longest Hatred*, Methuen, 1991.

RABBINIC PERIOD

Mishnah 'Avot (Ethics of the Fathers),   found in Daily Prayer Book.

Babylonian Talmud, ed., I. Epstein, Soncino, 1935–48.

Midrash Rabbah (10 vols.)   trans. H. Freedman and M. Simon, Soncino, 1939.

Midrash on Psalms (2 vols.)   trans. W. G. Braude, Yale University Press, 1959.

Pesikta de-Rab Kahana   trans. W. G. Braude & I. J. Kapstein, Routledge & Kegan Paul, 1975.

149

Pesikta Rabbati (2 vols.) trans. W. G. Braude, Yale University Press, 1968.

Bialik, H. N. & Ravnitzky, Y. N. (eds.) The Book of Legends, trans. W. G. Braude, Schocken/Kuperard, 1993.

Steinsaltz, A. The Talmud: A Reference Guide, Random House, 1989.

Urbach, E. E. The Sages: Their Concepts and Beliefs (2 vols.), trans. I. Abrahams, Magnes Press, 1979.

MEDIAEVAL PERIOD

Halevi, J. (1075–1141) The Kuzari: An Argument for the Faith of Israel, Schocken, 1987.

Maimonides, M. (1135–1204) Guide of the Perplexed (2 vols.), trans. S. Pines, Chicago University Press, 1975.

Pearl, C. Rashi, Weidenfeld & Nicolson, 1988.

Saperstein, M. Decoding the Rabbis: A Thirteenth Century Commentary on the Aggadot, Harvard University Press, 1980.

Sirat, C. A History of Jewish Philosophy in the Middle Ages, Cambridge University Press, 1985.

MYSTICISM

Sefer Yetzirah: The Book of Creation trans. A. Kaplan, S. Weiser, 1990.

The Bahir trans. A. Kaplan. S. Weiser, 1979.

The Wisdom of the Zohar ed. I. Tishby, trans. D. Goldstein, Littman Library, Oxford University Press, 1987.

Idel, M. Kabbalah: New Perspectives, Yale University Press, 1988.

Idel, M. Golem: Jewish Magical and Mystical Traditions on the Artifical Anthropoid, State University of New York Press, 1990.

Scholem, G. G. Major Trends in Jewish Mysticism, 2nd ed., Schocken, 1954.

Scholem, G. G. On the Kabbalah and its Symbolism, trans. R. Manheim, Schocken, 1965.

POST-MEDIAEVAL AND MODERN PERIOD

Berkovitz, E. Jewish Women in Time and Torah, Ktav, 1990.

Faur, J. Golden Doves with Silver Dots, Indiana University Press, 1986.

Gilbert, M. Atlas of the Holocaust, Weidenfeld & Nicolson, 1982.

Handelman, S. The Slayers of Moses: The Emergence of Rabbinic

Interpretation in Modern Literary Theory, State University of New York Press, 1982.

Hertzberg, A. (ed). *The Zionist Idea*, Atheneum, 1973.

Heschel, A. J. *God in Search of Man*, Jewish Publication Society, 1959.

Heschel, A. J. *The Sabbath: Its Meaning for Modern Man*; Jewish Publication Society, 1951.

Hirsch, S. R. *Collected Writings of Samson Raphael Hirsch* (6 vols.), Feldheim, 1984-90.

Jacobs, L. *Hasidic Thought*, Behrman House, 1976.

Kook, A. I. *The Lights of Penitence* etc., trans. Ben Zion Bokser, SPCK, 1979.

Lamm, N. *Faith and Doubt*. Ktav, 1986.

Levinas, E. *Nine Talmudic Readings*, trans. A. Aronowicz, Indiana University Press, 1990.

Michener, J.A. *The Source*, Secker & Warburg, 1965.

Rose, A. *Judaism and Ecology*, Cassell, 1992.

Soloveitchik, J. B. *Halakhic Man*, The Jewish Publication Society of America, 1983.

Weiss, A. *Women at Prayer*, Ktav, 1990.

Werblowsky, R. J. Z. *Joseph Karo: Lawyer and Mystic*, 2nd ed., Jewish Publication Society, 1977.

INDEX